FUCK YOU MARKETING

PS I Love You

Cassie Roma

**CR
& Co.**

FOREWORD

If you're reading this forward, then that means you've picked up a little piece of light, insight, truth, and creativity all wrapped up into a neat & highly recognizable package (ahem, a book).

Having known Cassie for a long time now, I can say - hand on heart - that never expected anything less from her when it comes to taking a "first rip" at writing a book.

You see, Cass's approach to life (as well as to marketing & advertising), has always been akin to a breath of fresh air on a particularly stifling hot day. Well, fresh air & an eye-roll-worthy Dad Joke timed just right.

As such, I can guarantee the contents of this book will be the same for you. A sweet breath in, & a gfaw of a laugh out. Especially if you're tired of drowning in marketing slang phrases like "thumb-stopping" & "snackable content." SOMEONE SAVE US FROM OURSELVES!

If you're the kind of person who likes to read real words that say really insightful things without the typical layer of *bullshit* added (am I allowed to write *bullshit* in a forward? Whoops. *Bullshit.* I wrote it three times because good things, memorable things come in threes.)

When I met Cass she was my boss. TBH, I didn't foresee the journey we've been on together - moving from colleagues to friends, & then to chosen family. But, that's just what happened with us.

With her, I learned how to craft and create stories that matter. I learned to treat poeple & their stories with kindness and compassion. Most importantly, I learned to craft a narrative whilst laughing my butt off the entire time.

I credit most of what I know about storytelling to Cass (the rest I can credit to those gritty lessons that we all learn through failure.)

The need to tell meaningful stories definitely became more important during the absolute sh*tshow that was 2020. I survived thanks to stories. I reckon we all did.

Stories of people helping each other when they could have only helped themselves. Stories of brands & people finally taking a stand for what's right over what's easy or given. And ,the stories of humanity learning that maybe, just maybe, there's more that brings us together than there is that divides us.

This book, I already know, will be a catalyst for some of the greatest stories that are yet to be told. Because at the end of the day, advertising folx & marketers are storytellers first.

So now that you've picked up the book, settle in. Enjoy the ride. And after you've read it, go and tell the best stories of your life— just like Cassie taught me to do.

With Love & SHAKAS!

Clare Cheyne
December, 2020

This book is dedicated to storytellers, dreamers, creators, & connectors.

You're my favorite kinds of humans.

Here's to changing the game so that we can break the rules over & over & over again.

CONTENTS

INTRODUCTION & APOLOGY

An Introduction & Apology (for all of the bull-shit I'm about to share with you)

Absurdity comes in all shapes & sizes. And, no, I'm not talking about my sartorial choices & fluctuating waistline.

Sometimes it makes itself known in big moments. Moments where we arrive at the finish line of a professional accomplishment, only to realize we've been running a marathon on a hamster wheel. The feeling of accomplishment is real—you've gone the distance—but the journey wasn't as beautiful as you'd imagined, right?

Well, duh: while focusing on one measure of accomplishment, we oftentimes forget the beauty of a fuller, deeper experience. Just imagine running that same distance near the ocean: the sound of waves crashing, seagulls calling your name, & palm trees cheering you on from above. No more hamster wheels.

While absurdity makes itself known in big moments of clarity, it thrives in small moments of in-between space. Almost undetectable, the absurd nature of our collective daily toil takes time to bubble to the surface. But it's there & we all start to notice it over time—on our own time.

Take a look around you now. Can you see it? It thrives in nuance, in side-eye glances from close colleagues, in awkward giggles at completely inappropriate times around executive boardroom tables.

We're all guilty of being blind to it at times, too. We believe (yes, we GODDAMN REALLY BELIEVE) that the work we're doing to bring/market/sell the world's most amazing thingamajig is worthy of our time, effort, passion, creativity, & skillsets. We forget to look up, look out, or look inward, & we often get all wrapped up in important shit that isn't really important to anyone else. This is why marketers really are a different breed of professional animal.

We're simultaneously completely focused on what we need to achieve & simultaneously clueless about much of the absurdity we bring to the world.

When it comes to absurdity, there are times when we're able to spot it from a million miles off. Like a flashing red light in the distance that gets closer & closer. As much as we try to avoid the light, we can't block it out or tip-toe around it. We careen towards it, out of control. Absurdity alarm bells squeal out a cringeworthy siren song that permeates our skulls and shouts, "run away while you can!"

But we can't run from it. We can't escape it. Friends, we're in too deep. We've got too much skin in the game. We're too far gone. We are too far gone...

Yep, we're all in the same weird professional twilight zone here. We all get sucked into the crazy on the daily.

No matter what we do, we can't get away from marketing's absurdity. We cover our ears, close our eyes, & hope against hope that the bright lights & screeching din will, at some point, become a beautiful melody we can dance to. But we're not dancers, dammit. Not at work, anyhow.

Though, if you're keen for some terrifyingly amazing moves, give me enough tequila & I become Swan Lake & a country music line dancing queen all in one small package. Yee haw & pip-pip.

My point is this: absurdity catches up with us. It sidles right up, does one of those sultry little bum-bump things where hips gently meet hips unexpectedly, then looks us in the eye (ever smiling), & spins us stories that—on weaker days—we take as truth.

Goddammit, why do we fall for it every time!?! I don't know. But I have good news: this isn't a weaker day & we're not going to believe the BS inherent in the absurdity of the game we play for one moment, are we? Nope, not today. We're not gonna believe it. We're going to stay rational, relatable, real. Of course we are.

We're smart, independent, free-thinking, rip-roaring, rollicking rides of a human beings. Which means, right here and right now, that we're in the right headspace to move forward with this book as a group of well-heeled humans.

The stories I'm about to tell you aren't meant to change your mind on anything. Seriously, they're not. They're merely meant to be a looking glass of sorts. A mirror reflection to step through & a new world in which we can openly giggle at ourselves.

What is this journey ahead of you all about?
It's hard to put into words. And, yes, I see the irony in saying this as it's exactly what I'm attempting to do. FFS, Roma, you're writing a book, after all!

In the pages ahead we're going to talk about jargon, influencers, assholes, the eradication of the colour orange, & raps that don't rhyme. We're also going to talk about trade secrets, strategic decision-making, and every other little ounce of bullshit we can dive into together while still remaining magically optimistic about the fantastic work we do as a collective. We'll spend time laughing at ourselves while recounting stories about how bloody hard we work to try to feel *less colouring-in* and *more superhero*.

That's right, I'm spilling some beans here.
A big 'ol can of them.

Or as my pre-teen just told me "It's spilling the tea, Mum. As in *big, juicy, tea.*" Okay, whatever, kid. Also, I added the *big,* juicy bit. Ha ha.

Regardless of what's being spilled (tea, beans, secrets) we're about to get the 411 on the DL.

When we reach the end of this book (hell, when we reach the end of this page), I hope we all leave having learned a thing or three about marketing, humanity's predisposition for complicating the simple, and having laughed a few good belly laughs along the way.

When it comes down to it, we're marketers.
We're the dreamers, the storytellers, & the creatives putting words, art, & ideas out into the world at scale. When we take ourselves too seriously, we lose the fun of what we do.
I'd like to highlight the fun here. The optimistic side of work & life.

In fact, if you snort-laugh at any point, please mark the spot in the book & tweet me with specifics.

My life goal is to bring people joy/horror in the form of Dad Jokes or dry humour that falls well short of being actually funny —thus, my personal key performance indicator of success is measured in snorts.

Right now, I'd like to thank you for picking up this book.

I appreciate it.

I'd also like to apologize.
There's a whole helluva lot to chew through together ahead.

Enjoy, Team!
Or not.

You do you, Boo.

ALARMING/ODD

When my wife asked me, "What will the first chapter of your book be?" my immediate response was "The one that comes before any other, obvs!" Quickly followed by, "Also, it'll be chapter directly preceding the second."

Needless to say, eyes rolled (not mine).
Snort laughs happened (okay, yes, mine).
And both the tone & sass level for this chapter were immediately set to: DEFCON LEVEL, HIGH.

You, dear reader, can probably garner from the title of this chapter, that we're starting this book off with a bang. You see, I need to come clean from the get-go and let you know that am a reluctant, and quite accidental, marketer. In fact, I actively try to *not* label myself as a marketer (or to allow others to do it for me). Yet, it still happens.

That said, I am many things and define myself by many a label, but "marketer" doesn't make the Top 10 List. Here we are though, traversing a familiar landscape together that is all about marketing. Again, the irony is not lost on me at all.

Why is it, you may wonder, that I am oftentimes hell-bent on being known as anything other than a marketer? Well, mostly because the last 15 years of my professional life are not what I'd imagined they'd be when I dipped my toes into the churning, beautiful, deep ocean of adulting.

A push & pull of tides that seem to work without a direct pull from the moon's gravitational field, the waves upon which my career & personal life have ridden are always without direct course. Which means I've had to learn to swim, surf, sail, & simply hold on for dear life as I've grown into who I am today. The tides are forever changing, which means I have forever been learning to enjoy whichever way they've taken me.

But, back in the beginning, just out of college, newly married, & with a small child, I realised that a lady-that-lunches lifestyle wasn't something I could afford to be—on more levels than one. First, we didn't have a lot of money, which meant that I needed to work to provide for my young family. I've always believed in being able to make my own way in the world & was completely cool with working to provide.

Also, with little cash to apportion to "extravagances" the last thing I wanted was to be eating all of my extra dough. Second, I've never had a lot of time for surface level banal conversations in which being part of some in-crowd was a status level badge I needed to achieve to feel chuffed with myself.

Thus, a Lunching Lady I was never meant to be.

So, it was that, in my early twenties, I started looking for a job (ahem, not a career) that allowed me to

...

a) pay the bills
b) utilise at least a tiny amount of my creative & strategic skills/ passions whilst on the job and
c) look forward just far enough in the future to know I could evolve as a human while doing better by others.

Marketing ticked most of the boxes I've just mentioned.
So, I jumped in before checking the water.

7

Luckily, it was deep enough and I knew how to tread water well enough.

I'm sure glad I jumped in, too. Because having zero expectations around the guardrails of a job title meant that I went into my working life with rose-coloured glasses on. Hell yes, here's to a good dose of daily positivity & reckless optimism, both of which I have stored up in spades for days that are more glum than glam.

As someone who has always had a creative lilt to my speech and a strategic hitch in my get-along, marketing seemed (and still does seem like) a good place to start down the road of professional life as a woman who is both a thinker & a dreamer.

My first *real job* in marketing wasn't a marketing job at all. My title was Assistant Operations Manager at a 24-hour gym company, & it was in this first role that I learned a lot about the behind-the-scenes stuff that makes truly remarkable professionals who they are.

I spent most of my days greeting gym junkies & sweaty Bettys. Getting to know each person, their schedules, their quirks, the things that drove them to run for an hour every day or to life Hulk-like weights, or to sweat their guts out in spin classes three times a week. I knew which protein powder they liked. Knew the music they preferred to have pumped through the sound-system at 3am & learned how to banter in a million different ways with a million different people to create emotive connections with them.

This daily interaction with people who were as different as they were similar established in me a firm foundation in how brands should (and, by rights, shouldn't) interact with their customers. More on that later though.

What I soon learned was that time taken to know and tell stories, to chit-chat, & the care taken in adding a personal touch to an interaction always resulted in more time in the gym for our members. And thus, more time resulted in more money changing hands over the counter when it came to moving our big-brand items in the Pro Shop.

Looking back on it, though it didn't seem it at the time while I was re-stocking vending machines, cleaning up other people's sweat from fitness machines, or attending to a "Code Brown" in the showers, I was learning the most important rule in the game of marketing: connect with people first, don't hard-sell to them. Tell them stories, get to know them, build trust, make them giggle.

Then, & only then, will they keep coming back.
Then & only then, will they love buying more from you more often.

Other foundational marketing skills that I learned in this job were:

Truth:
Always tell the truth—especially at work. If you fuck something up (and believe me, you will fuck things up often if you're worth your weight in salt & stay curious), own your fuck-up. When you're able to quickly own up to a mistake or miscommunication, others learn from the get-go that you're trustworthy & won't be throwing them under any proverbial (or real) busses.

If I've learned anything over the past two decades as someone working in a fast-moving & creative field, it's that telling the truth is sometimes the hardest thing to do. But it's the best thing to do. It's easier to avoid hard conversations than it is to face them head-on, but the more honest you can be about things both big and small, the longer & more illustrious (ahem, maybe even enjoyable) your career will be. The truth, well, it'll set you (& me—all of us!) free.

Constructive feedback

My "ah ha!" moment concerning feedback comes less from a customer-facing (social media community management) perspective than one between colleagues, managers, & shitty bosses who obviously never learned that feedback has to be constructive for it to be actionable.

I absolutely love the idea of Ye Olde Positivity Sandwich & apply this tasty strategy to my own leadership lunchbox. To build one, first, you start with a slice of positivity. Like Wonder Bread itself, your first sentence or opening statement to someone should be something that sets up your conversation for success. Starting with a positive piece of feedback, then leading into the meat of your conversation, makes sure that this layer of your positivity sandwich is palatable & clearly outlines solutions or ways to improve a project or situation.

Be clear, too. Speak simply, succinctly, & without and creative swirls of industry slang. Why? Because, clear is kind. Once the meat/protein/constructive clarity is added to you Positivity Sandwich, it's time to add another slice of positivity for reinforcement. Viola! Constructive feedback served with dill pickles & a side of crunchy Ranch flavoured chips. The best!

One thing to note here: there are a lot of folks out there in all industries who take any feedback as a personal attack. Society has conditioned us to think that, unless people are telling us that the sun shines out of our own cabooses, that they're telling us to fuck off. This is mind boggling to me. The best thing any of us can do is to put ourselves into rooms where we're the least knowledgeable person. That's where we really grow, learn, & evolve. PB&J, anyone?

Kindness

Kindness MUST be the foundation upon which you build your life & your career. Sure, go ahead, be a kick-ass, take-no-shit, hard-as-nails marketeer (yeah, go ahead and call yourself a marketeer, it's a bit piate-like which sounds kinda cool) with awards up the wazoo—but don't burn every goddamn bridge along the way to get there.

Sure, the pathway to hell (& to fame in the marketing game) might be paved with good intentions and a drive to give back to the world, but if you're an asshole about it, you'll not only die alone on your hill of awards, but there won't even be a single, quirky ECD around at your funeral to pay tribute to your contributions to creative clickbait. Over the years, I've been teased for being kind. Weird, right?

I've also been flat-out called a fantasist for believing that better days might just be ahead whilst going through hard times. Being nice doesn't equate to weakness though. It never has & never will. The grittiest, most nuanced, most deeply loved & respected leaders in the game have one thing in common: kindness. The rest is noise. Beautiful, awkward, imperfect, meaningful, meaningless, fun, shitty, annoying, sweet noise.

Silliness at all junctures
For chrissakes, we're marketers. We're not flying the planes whose seats we're working our asses off to fill with others asses. We're not saving lives pushing dirty retail tactics & moving consumer goods. We are not the essential workers who keep the world spinning and life moving onward. Our job as marketers is to add a bit of fun, purpose, interestingness, & silliness back into the world.

If we're good at what we do, we connect with others while we grow the bottom line for shareholders. We're frowny-faced facilitators of insight & outcome most of the time, though. SMILING? WTAF is a smile at work. WE ARE SERIOUS PROFES-

SIONALS IN FLORAL SUITS DAMMIT! Lord forbid we cross from serious to silly, aye?

I remember listening to a CMO speak in a meeting once where we were reporting on end of quarter results. The fact of the matter was that the numbers weren't good. The lines that we wanted to see moving up & to the right on our pivot tables were heading left & downward. In a moment, the CMO said our "negative growth in sales was driven by a slowing market." If you're in Marketing Land all of the damn time, you might not see anything wrong with that sentence.

But he (being a hilarious, lovely man) & I both did—& we laughed out loud together. "Boss, you just said *negative growth*" instead of a "decrease" in sales. First off, I offered him a quick golf clap for his instantaneous shuffling of language to make something that should sting like a bee feel more like a tickle from a daisy. Secondly, I had to give him a "well freaking done you, Big Boy," for laughing at his own bullshit-spinning in real time.

To be able to laugh at ourselves and the little kingdoms we build in big business is important. Silliness is necessary ALL OF THE DAMN TIME if you're going to survive the marketing and advertising world. Park your ego. Laugh. Seriously, when you can see a moment for what it is, laugh. When you can't see a moment as anything other that Twilight Zone-esque, laugh louder. You live one life and might as well enjoy it, regardless of the never-ending colloquialisms, the reams of big data that exist only to drown in, and the fuzzy insights you hold as self-evident truths.

Now, there's an *alarming* story I'd like to share with you. I haven't told many people about this, so why not make it as public as hell when I do, right? Seems like a life strategy that's worked for me thus far – so lessgo!

This story is about the *oddest* email I've ever seen. Ever. And believe you me, I have received some real zingers over the years. To be honest, I've sent my fair share, too. If there was an award ceremony for the most shocking electronic communications ever sent thought, the email I'm about to share with you would be a Grand Finalist.

You know those pivotal moments in your life that you look back on & think, "Wow, *THAT* was the moment that helped me pivot in my career" or "*THAT* was the turning point that helped me become a better human,"? This wasn't one of those. Soz.

When I opened aforementioned zinger of an email, it looked normal. Standard. Safe enough. But, I knew from the moment my eyes started taking in the words on a digital page in front of me that this email was different.

The words that looked like English felt like slanguage & then my stomach fell as my mind untangled the intent of the message. No hindsight was needed to grasp the weight of inherent craziness that came together in sentences and paragraphs. No tether was needed to keep the clouds nearer to the ground on this one. Nuh uh. This was full-tilt loco lighting up my inbox.

If I'm honest, this *alarming & odd* exchange sent me into one helluva mental tizzy. So shooketh was my mind that I decided to write this book. YES! A single e-mail made me want to WRITE A BOOK. But...why?

Because in the course of one subject line, two paragraphs, & a sign-off for the ages, everything about the ego involved in marketing became clear to me.

What I was experiencing in the moment was akin to the calm you feel after a near-death experience: your life has flashed before your eyes and you know what's important now. If you're like me and have been through what I call a "pre-middle age unravelling" (ahem, existential crisis, anyone?), this e-mail was the button someone literally pushed that brought me a bucket-load of mental clarity. Folks, this was the pinnacle of marketing crazy.

This was my weird e-mail Everest.
I'd reached the peak of professional cray-cray & everything else ahead was bound to be downhill.

I won't give you all of the dirty details here word-for-word, but here's the crux of the clearly cobbled-together communication: after seeing the colour orange in a photo, a brand manager in a big business LOST HER SHIT. LOST IT! She had seen a photo of a human wearing something orange (a competitor brand's main hue) in an image & wanted it removed from ALL THE THINGS. And I mean *allthegoddamnthings.*

Orange was to be removed from the world. Orange was to be eradicated.
The eradication of organe was being tabled. Literally.
This included, but was not limited to, already existing orange things, Photoshop logos, the universe, human eyesight, & definitely from the photo in question.

Yep, the ENTIRETY OF THE COLOUR ORANGE needed to disappear. Why? Well, in ways described as both *alarming* & *odd,* this unicorn of a wayward brand marketer believed that waving a magic wand & getting rid of any reference to another brand's colour would immediately make her brand stronger by default. Someone shake me. Even writing this now, my eyes are rolling nearly out of my head.

You see, sometimes brand people get so into their jobs (and yes, I have been guilty of this a time or two as well) that we forget there's a world outside of the teeny tiny brand or logo that we work with daily. All of the deep meaning imbued into a drop-shadow, the soul inherent in a variant of lavender, or the full stop at the end of a slogan is almost always unnoticed by most normal humans. I mean, take your marketing hat off, & WHO

THE FUCK CARES ABOUT YOUR PASSIONATE DROP SHADOW?
Not me.

But we marketers, we're not normal humans, are we?

So it goes that the person who wrote this email decided that a
competitor's colour needed to be erased from the human colour
palate. As much as I hate to spread rumors, rumor has it that this
woman also refused to allow her four children to wear orange to
school!

ERMERGERHD are you freaking kidding me?
Get rid of a colour?
Punish your kids?
Seriously, if we all stepped back for a minute and pondered on
this *alarming & odd* conundrum, could we even imagine a world
without orange?

What would sunsets be like without orange?
How would we spot Dutch people in their national garb?
What about Ernie?
Would Bert have loved him as much, had he not been the perfect
shade of orange?
And how about most citrus fruits?

No, no.
Honey, no.
We NEED ORANGE in this world.

In fact, we need to start looking at marketing as more than a
brand book, a manifesto, a series of rules and established tem-
plated norms that should never be molded, amended, evolved,
or otherwise fucked with. Team, we need to be open to the pos-
sibility of a changing world in which marketing is now malle-
able.

We cannot shout at consumers & tell them what our brands
mean. We must imbue everything we do, share, say, and sell

15

with meaning. And we must allow actual humans who work and shop with us to tell their stories—while offering them opportunities to weave us into the core of who they fundamentally believe themselves to be.

Simon Sinek talks about playing the *infinite game* in life & in business. By realizing that you cannot win at brand, you cannot win at business, & you cannot win at erasing an entire colour from the palate of life, you strategically choose the long game. In doing so, you choose a lifetime of fun, wonder, weirdness, & self-made success.

In fact, I reckon the marketers who play a forever game of self-improvement & fear not the colour of a competitor infringing upon their brand territory are those who will most immediately & obviously rise to the top. No matter how alarming or odd we find something, it is those who find both the beauty and the beast in the absurdity of our colouring in departments that last.

What do you reckon, dear reader?
Do you see this, too?

SLANGUAGE &
SATURDAYS

N ow that we're all grounded in some of the absurdities that bring our lives as professional marketers/creatives/agency peeps into bright, glittery, gritty, nuanced neon light, it seems the right time to speak simply, openly. Using words of the same ilk, too. I'm going to try my absolute damndest to not fill these pages with wanky ineptitudes or strategic slanguage meant to distract from the simplicity of our actual jobs-to-do on the daily.

When we boil marketing right down to it, our role as marketers of all kinds is to entertain, inform, educate, & otherwise offer value to people. Value, my friends, is the only true currency of business. From the beginning of modern human civilization (& I imagine even beforehand, when we were cave painting, nomadic, huntresses & hunters in kick-ass loincloths), an exchange had to be valued on both sides. If one party didn't see the inherent quality in a trade, then the trade didn't happen. It's that simple.

Somewhere, we tried to get a bit too clever, though. Didn't we? We started to think that, because we (those with big budgets & the ability to utilize media on a macro, mass-market scale) could tell others about the value of our product or service, they'd listen. They wouldn't question. And for a long time, this was akin to the truth. Those who held the purse strings were able to create unquestionable narratives that nodded to value, but most of the time delivered very little.

In our modern media age, an age where attention is our most valuable asset, we're re-learning how to return actual value not only to our customers, but to society as a whole. Why? Well, when we add value to the lives of others (be it in ways big or small), it is then & only then that others begin to trust, understand, & like our brand enough to choose us when it's time to buy whatever it is that we're peddling.

All of this leads me to the importance of words and language. Without them, we don't have a narrative, and consumers can't make sense of their own narrative and where we might fit into who they believe they are.

When we're talking to the public, communicating a benefit of our brand, or creating something wiz-bang to put out into the world (hell, even when we're writing copy for the most banal of dirty 'ol P&P ads for OOO), we use simple, impactful words. We have to. Consumers are clued-up, deeply engaged, & over being told what they should believe.

Luckily, we're not only marketers, we're also normal humans (at least on the weekend), so we understand this. And we work bloody hard to ensure the words we chose matter.

So why is it that we start speaking a foreign language when we head to work? The language we speak is slightly lyrical but lacks rhyme. When non-marketers or non-office-saddled-jockeys hear us in our native environments, they frown. Eyebrows furrowed, eyes wide open in wild wonder, quietly pondering, "What in the hell am I listening to? Is this a secret society way of communicating? What am I missing here? Can anyone in this damn room just speak to me like a normal person?"

You're nodding along as you read this, aren't you? I am nodding while writing this. And as much as it pains me to admit it, I've been called out multiple times by my daughter, my friends outside of the marketing world, & even some colleagues across varying marketing professions for forgetting myself & falling into a marketing parlance out of context.

So why in the world are we, as a collective, so committed to a slanguage amongst ourselves that in normal day-to-day life means naught to many? I have a few theories (some tested, others simply deduced from 16 years of watching others).

First, the *why*. Yep, I'm going to get all Simon Sinek on you here. I think the reason we speak in an array of marketing tongues is (yep, I'm going to be blunt here) to make what is inherently simple complex. The truth of the matter is that nothing we do, & I mean nothing, is rocket science. If it was, we'd have perfected understanding the beautiful irrationality of human behavior, & we'd spend most of our time telling stories, creating innate bonds, and driving connections that matter.

As it is, we over-pivot when it comes to the science of what we do over the craft of it. How often do you roll your eyes or otherwise feel the urge to tear your hair out when you have both your media agency and your creative agency in a room? (All the while praying that, for once, they'll play nice and conjure magic.)

For me, a lot of the vernacular is wrapped around a need to justify ourselves. Traditional business people like to place marketers in a bucket that doesn't include depth of strategic thinking. We're teased about being the Colouring-In Department, and have to exaggerate the fact that we understand other departments of the machine we're working in. I mean, not to toot our own proverbial horn, but c'mon, we are literally the people who exist to make a business, product, idea, or persona shine.

We are here for the depth, the fun, the entertainment, & the foundations of brand strength. Without these things, there'd be no finance department. There'd be no insights and data. There'd be no digital team. There'd be no business. Yes! I went there. Disbelievers, fight me on it. I dare ya.

In the midst of attempting to prove our worth beyond having a desk drawer full of Crayolas or Sharpies to draw unintelligible squiggles on unlined artsy paper, we started building a vernacular of words that made us sound much more complex than we needed to. Our Insider's Language, much like those of the finance folks, the operating crew, & the exec sweethearts, aligned us more as true professionals.

But I think it's also worked against us. By puffing up our own self-worth through throw-away words, and by trying to win at slang one-upmanship, we've left behind our love for actual humans. We've forgotten how to take off our marketing hats in a workplace, and we often outclever even ourselves. This isn't ideal, Team.

Now that I've talked about *why* I think we use slanguage so often, I'd like to nod to how often we speak like this. If I start from the very beginning (the very best place to start), I'd say this: sunup to sundown. That's when we talk like goofballs. Whether it's in meetings, greetings, or moments so fleeting, we fall into our tribe's silo.

We speak in riddles about engagement, about return on investment, about customer sentiment, & about laddering up our strategic objectives to ensure we leverage the correct vertical targeting across demographics. Online, offline, in line, and everywhere else we can, we try & make it seem like we know all of the things about all of the channels & about all of the individual traits that make customers either like us or not.

We SPEAK IN CODE. And we need to stop. Seriously. Half a decade ago, the hot buzzword was "viral." I couldn't even pee in peace without someone asking me how to ensure their campaign, their product, their idea, or their bland corporate-jargony video would go viral. Ahem, then as to now, virality is equal parts value, entertainment, FOMO, and hyper-relevance.

Oh yeah, you need a sprinkle of good luck thrown in for good measure to drive your main measures, too. Now the word "content" is thrown around like glitter at a unicorn convention. My job is to ensure we all start speaking more clearly. As the amazing Brené Brown has said, *"clear is kind."* And as a self-appointed Kindness Warrior, I'm here to ask questions that help marketers & colleagues beyond marketing delve into cleverness underpinned by simple, well-crafted, messages, & strategies.

To be clearer, kinder even, I have come up with a few ways to stop the onslaught of slanguage in our beloved profession. May we lead the way back to the light for the younger generations of marketers, those who suckled from Mother Social Media and who know naught but a world with an open internet and many closed doors.

HOW TO STOP SPEAKING MARKETING SLANG IN 3 EASY STEPS:

Talk like a 12yr old

This is not just a work lesson, but a life lesson. We marketers are known for praying at the Altar of Busy. We deify the state of being busy. We try to be the first person in the office & the last to leave, just to prove our worth. Somewhere along the line, we forgot that actual outputs and results matter more than wasting your life away at a plank of wood.

So it goes, if your kid has to stop you midsentence & says "Mom, I don't understand anything you're saying about hacking algorithms by understanding the cultural significance of memes & other zeitgeist moments," then you, like me, need a little slap up the side of the head. It is so much more difficult to speak con-

21

cisely and to be single-minded in focus— so if you're looking to really impress me (or anyone else, for that matter), spend less time on delivering more & think through your words, rather than opening a faucet just to watch the water run.

Be Clear... clear is kind.
I'm just going to leave this one right here, as it is.

CLEAR.
IS.
KIND.

Momma Brené Brown teaches this daily in her talks/books/ interviews on communication. Don't distort the beauty of clarity by filling the spaces between with words that are a dime a dozen. Allow silence to speak; make meaningful words your workhorses. Allow clarity to become your BFF.

Go back to the beginning.
If you treat people like they're not smart enough to see through your heartless bullshit, then you're already on the backfoot & always will be. Consumers & colleagues alike are smart, but they're also human.

We all are, & that's the best thing we have going for us right now. We know that the science of influence is such that we think others can easily be led by the crowd or the cool new thing— but we don't see ourselves being just as influenced. Right here & now, I am throwing down a challenge to you—yes, you. The next time you're in a meeting & realize that everyone around you is talking in circles of marketing nonsense, pull people up.

Speak like you would on Saturdays.

KOOL-AID & XANAX

If you're in the marketing game for the long run, you're going to need to know a few things. First, rickety old roller-coasters are pussy-cats compared to the ride you're about to embark/continue/stay on. The only purring you're going to experience is more akin to whirring while you run at the pace of cultural & technological change.

In human terms: the profession you've chosen isn't just a moving feast, it's a Ferrari ride of a cornucopia. If you're going to last, you'll need to learn to pace yourself & to put different ingredients together to build taste-sensations of sorts.

Marketing is more than getting people to like your brand enough to buy whatever ware it is you're peddling—it's a constant sprint at the pace of changing culture. The quicker you learn to love the pace of change, the quicker you find your own rhythm. Personally, the thing I love most about marketing as a profession is that I get paid to understand humans as fallible, beautiful creatures driven by ego, identity, & empathy. In understanding others, I understand myself more.

And with all of this understanding built into the foundation of who I'm evolving into, I have the immense honor of helping to craft stories that move people. Stories that match & help to evolve amazing new & existing platforms.

Let's talk about platforms for a minute (or five).

At times, the platforms we utilize to reach consumers seem light-years ahead of our collective ability to adapt to them creatively. It's as if we have visions in our heads of how we'd love to tell a certain story, but we can't yet find the code, words, or visuals to be able to do so.

By rights, we push forward without knowing whether our stories will emerge perfectly into the world. We make peace with what could very well be imperfect. Hell, we might screw up so badly that we fall on our faces & no one even notices the passion & toil we put out into the world. This is the conundrum of modernity.

Technology & humanity are forever intertwined. Forever dancing a tentative tango. Yet, we dance. And we fall into step, too. Though at other times, the inverse is true. We, as creative sentient beings, can also sprint past technology with our abilities to see art in places where once we believed that art did not exist. This is our magic.

No AI or machine learning, ever, will see art where it has never been seen. That kind of life exists only behind human eyes. Even so, we've been hoodwinked for at least a decade now into thinking that social media is art. That digital is the be-all & end-all. We're speeding through the beauty.

And it's been quite a trip, eh?! So, right now, I ask you to hold on tight. Buckle up. Batten the hatches, me hearties. For a long career in marketing (hell, even for a short-lived one), you're going to need uppers & downers in equal measure. We're quite a diverse bunch, but we're really all one big, quirky, happy family. And being family means that we're all in this together: <INSERT BATTLE CRIES OF KICK-ASS MARKETERS HERE>.

If you're like me, you've looked at others in our profession (usually from competitor brands) & said "Sheesh, that person is cray-cray! What a load of BS. They're obviously drinking their own Kool-Aid."

While I'm not at all advocating for anyone to do anything as silly as lace their own drinks or the drinks of anyone else with something that will fog a person's ability to think for themselves, it'd be remiss of me to not point out just how susceptible we all are to believing our own spin. We're spreadsheet warriors & sprinters with no finish line in sight. It's time we drop the act. It's time we start to question everything, from our media spend to our creative executions. Why? Because there's a glut of boring marketing flooding markets. And boring marketing is beige. It's a waste of all of our time. We need to stop creating shit that doesn't need to be created at all in the first place.

With this in mind, I should define Kool-Aid in the context of our profession (any profession, really). In the real world, Kool-Aid is a sugar-laden, brightly coloured drink used by parents to hype up their little ones at birthday parties. It's such a sweet mixture that, when served ice cold on a summer's day, you might actually think you're sipping ambrosia. In marketing, though, it's different altogether. In marketing, it's a mask.

Sweet on the tongue, the Kool-Aid we mix for ourselves promises us a sugar rush—but a sugar rush it is not. Lacking in any true nutritional or spiritual value, mixing, pouring, and drinking the Kool-Aid Is harmful. The Kool-Aid we drink as grown-ass professional adults is a poison that convinces us to believe our own bullshit. And if there's danger in anything, it's in believing one's own bullshit. When we don't continually practice self-reflection that is honest & gritty, our work suffers. We become monotone versions of ourselves. We learn to long for more & more of the sugar rush instead of finding adventure in newness, innovation, & true creativity.

Kool-Aid is what fortifies us & keeps us spouting crap like, "we can control the conversation." When we're buzzing on the juice, we think we're more important than our consumers. We believe in the folly that is thinking we cannot & should not be making a purposeful difference in the world.

But seriously, we have all been there. We've all happily sucked at our straws at the dinner table of marketing amazingness and drunk from the chalice of self-righteousness and fruit punch Kool-Aid. The pick-me-up inherent in imbibing is necessary sometimes to simply keep on keepin' on. The necessity for all of us is knowing when we've had enough to drink, & pushing the Kool-Aid away.

On the flip-side to the upper that is our marketing Kool-Aid, we also self-medicate with a form of professional Xanax. Now, I must note right here that Xanax itself is something that helps a lot of people when taken in accordance with a medical professional's prescription. When it comes to us marketers, though, I use the term loosely as something that calms our nerves, sedates us, & takes us a full 180 degrees away from the hyped way in which we operate when we're drinking our own Kool-Aid.

Just like Elvis, Johnny Cash, & Jerry Lee Lewis did, we need uppers & downers in equal measure to keep livin' our rock n roll advertising lifestyle, or so we think. Quite a large proportion of us truly believe that we're more informed & exceedingly cleverer than the hoi polloi [LP5] who consume the work we toil over. REALITY CHECK: we're not. In fact, when it comes down to it, we're more susceptible to marketing. We speak in tongues that overcomplicate the simplistic. We pat ourselves on the back for jobs well done with trips to exotic beaches where we lust after awards that mean a whole lot of nothing.

Le sigh.
Someone pass me a Xanax, please.

The longer I'm in the proverbial game, the further I travel for work, & the more people I meet who are coming to terms with a common-sense approach to marketing that puts humans at the center of all of our work, the more I'm convinced that it's time to start going cold turkey when it comes to the Kool-Aid & the Xanax. We deserve to hop off the roller coaster for a little bit & take in the scenery around us. We deserve to calm a spinning head & re-learn how to sit in silence whilst allowing beautiful boredom to overcome us.

It's taken me a long time to realize that some high-quality H2O is the best thing for sippin' when working in this industry. Mixing up our own cup of self-delusion is just that... deluded (also, LOL, it's literally diluted). My best advice? Slow down. Study good work & work for good. Borrow strategy. Test out purpose-driven creative executions. Learn to love the learning moments that come from abject failure. And, more than anything, once the cloud of Kool Aid clears from your mind, dive deep into data & insight from which you can tell stories that stick.

This all might seem like a big heaping serving of eggs that I'm teaching you to suck. But I promise you, that's not my intention. My intent here is to call you out, to call me out, to call all of us out when it comes to believing the hype about the hype we created ourselves. Consumers don't care about our back-patting & our frenetic pace. The care only about how they feel after having interacted with our brands & products.

The rest?
It's all just noise.
Tropical fruit punch-flavoured noise.

CH-CH-CHANGING CHANNELS

Okay, okay, okay. I need to warn you about this chapter. It's gonna be a little bit sappy, maybe even a little on the saccharine sweet side of things when it comes to talking advertising & marketing.

Let's face it, marketers & ad people are basically geniuses of creating demand, telling stories, putting social movements into motion, & keeping the world turning. No seriously, we're pretty freaking awesome as a larger collective. Sure, we need number crunchers, we need money people, we need HR & people support, we need operational teams to keep big businesses running.

But, c'mon now, if we're completely honest & open to beating our chests a bit (honesty & openness means of course we all know we're open to being beaty-chesty at all times), without us, there'd be nothing. There'd be no pull. There'd be no one waiting in lines around entire New York City blocks for a new Apple phone to go on sale or for a new pair of Michael Jordan basketball shoes to drop. Why? Because we've been doing this for a long time: the selling of stories as a way of trading in social currency.

We're not one trick ponies, either. By rights, we're completely unafraid when it comes to the types of advertisements we're willing to tell our stories through. It is us who tell vast groups of people how to look, feel, live, & be. The power to do harm or good is strong— this is why there are such stringent laws & rules around what we can say, when we can say it, & where we can say it.

For the record, I'm all for rules & regulations, too. A few bad apples can really help rot to spread & can do harm without fear of reprisal. Thus, it's important that we continue to lift the colleagues & competitors we know who are pushing to do well for & by others. Marketing plays such a major role in how we define ourselves as individuals & as groups. It also tells us how we should move through the world. What a heady idea to ponder on. We're not just the goddamn coloring-in department. That's a small minded & jealous person's way of diminishing a group of people who've helped to define what our world is today.

Don't believe me? Think about it for a minute. Marketing is the front lines. The first touchpoint. The longest lasting memory. Simply put: with changing tides in how we live in a modern, tech-saturated world, it is on us to create & market products that shape a tenable & sustainable cultural outlook. With that, we build a hopeful generation, a lifetime of connection.

Right now, we have such a vast excess of media available compared to our needs. The last time I read the numbers, we were sitting at 2,500 minutes of content available for consumption to every 1 minute of human life on the planet. That's 2,499 minutes of advertising, storytelling, P&P shouty ads on TV, & ambient radio that will never be consumed. With the glut of content, as consumers, we are all powerful. We download ad blockers like there's no tomorrow.

We also all possess the most powerful ad blocker of all—one that needs no download—our minds. With a democratisation of content creation & distribution comes huge power. We can now choose. We can choose which content we engage with & which is simply noise that we dampen down until it's not even registering in the background of our consciousness. Which means as marketers, we need to really buckle down & dive deep into the business of meaning. Of being *meaningful.*

I often ask my colleagues if they believe that, even with all of the reporting, optimisation, & data at our fingertips, we're doing a good job in shifting the world away from dire consumerism towards a more sustainable & circular way of living. The answer is resoundingly, "No. Not even close." Le sigh. What gives?

In our modern media world of fast & open communication, we over-index & over-spend on reach because we assume eyeballs equal impact. They don't. Surely we can see that the rules have changed. Or rather, that there were never any rules to begin with. What matters most now is what has always mattered most: personal connection. We've all now come to a point in time at which all people inherently value less the contribution of any brand, personal brand, or product owner in bringing us content we don't need.

For a while, we didn't have a choice about the marketing we saw; it was dictated by the limited media we had. Less than 100 years ago, we had print media, radio, TV. The men who controlled these mediums controlled what we heard & saw. We were inundated, sure. But we weren't drowning. Right now we're all searching for the "off buttons." In fact, people are deleting channels instead of adding more to their already full lives. You need only to search "people deleting social media apps" & you'll get 40 million results served back to you in just over half a second. 40 million. I'd look at these results as 40 million reasons to get reacquainted with the beauty of the channels we have as marketing professionals & the ways in best to conjure magic through them.

What follows is a breakdown of the six super pillars of all traditional & emerging marketing campaigns. I ask you, as you read through these, to think deeply about how much time you're spending working on each channel, how you're working to bring these together in omnichannel or multichannel iterations, & where you truly find the sweet spot.

No two campaigns are the same, no two products are the same, & no two moments in time are the same. Therefore, mastering marketing is a fool's errand. Enjoying the wild ride? That's where I find immense joy.

Words, Mouths, Ideas

The first channel or avenue that I'm keen to talk to is my marketing Bae: **Word of Mouth Advertising.** Word of mouth is how we survive as a species. Through stories, tall tales, & superior sales pitches, we learn about the world around us. As children, we learn everything from morality & religion to how we should comport ourselves at all times through the humble fairy tale & fable.

Most of the cautionary tales we learn when we're little seep into our psyches without us ever questioning a single world or moral of the story. When we look at marketing, word of mouth isn't just the first form of advertising that existed, it's also still the most potent. I have good news for you, Dear Reader. Great news, even. Word of mouth (WOM) is HAWT again. And I mean smokin' hot. THANK FUCK for it, too!

We've been so blinded (potentially blindsided) by the smoke & mirrors of digital marketing that we've completely forgotten to treat humans like the cognisant, sentient beings that we all are. We've boiled consumers right down into a single data point. We've melded dreams, desires, & drive with sales as an end result & by-product of doing business well. Yuck.

Word of mouth, a.k.a. talking to other people, has been proven as the most impactful marketing channel in the entire world during the course of all time & across all of humankind. Why? Because honesty, trust, & safety are all inherently built into the things we say when we're with people we like. Whether it's hilarious shit-talking where we drop stories, anecdotes, or banter about a favourite brand or product, or if we're actually deep-diving into a pool of marketing fancy with colleagues or peers, we share because we want to look cool & we want to help people.

Word of mouth isn't a trigger we can pull or an algorithm we can hack. It's breath & mind coming together in a confluence of social currency as ideas & recommendations are shared between individuals. We're tired of the bullshit, the banality, & the throw-shit-at-a-wall & see what sticks approach... but to understand why we are where we are, we need to go back in time to celebrate marketing & the profound influence it has had/still has on all of our lives.

In the past year or so, I've noticed that word of mouth is coming back into focus as something that marketers & businesses alike need to spend more time nurturing. But this isn't happening at scale. For a while there (over a decade, Team, over a decade), we were blinded & bamboozled by promised riches & business success through digital ad placements & social media community insiders.

During this same time, some of us forgot to invest in reasons that cause people to care about our products. We didn't give love & attention to the power & importance that is inherent in giving people a reason to talk about us. It's selfish to simply expect customers to take in advertising information online & reshare it in an analogue way without forming true connections or embedding narratives strong enough to be taken in & reshared over time. It's crazy to think people care about our targeted banner ad as much as they care about feeding their families, raising kind children, or simply getting dinner onto the table.

Which brings me to WOM strategy. Some of the most brilliant word of mouth advertising isn't advertising at all. It's chit chat, banal banter, & dinnertime conversations that will never feature on a customer panel or an insights report that can either lift a brand or stop it in its tracks.

To drive conversations, the best strategy is to create them. By investing in memories, you'll be memorable. Simple, right? *insert wink emoji here because, yes, I realize I have completely just super-simplified a complex idea that deserves its very own book—roll with me here.* Call it what you will: WOM or talk-triggers or social currency. Whatever you do, I beg of you, start with word of mouth as the ultimate goal for your business & then work your way back towards more nuanced & tactical marketing plans. If you truly have your customer at the heart of what you do, you'll care more about what they say about you to others than any other like, share, re-tweet, or otherwise shallow show of liking something.

Print it Out & Get Out of Home
I'm merging print & out of home (OOO) platforms in this paragraph because I can. It seems to me that these two mediums (especially prior to digital billboards) work on a similar plane of creative being. By that, I mean that similar principles exist in best practices across both OOO & print advertising models. Case in point: you must have a good grasp of the native tongue of the consumers you're advertising to.

Also important, after grabbing said tongue, is being visually clear & concise with the layout of your ad. Notice how I didn't mention cleverness, but instead, "clear & concise." Quite often in print & billboard marketing, I find that we overreach on cleverness—so much so, that we miss the point we're trying to make in the first place. Clever has a place, sure. But clever is best when it happens naturally & when it is born of simple messaging. (More on that later.)

Let's change gears for a moment & shine a light on the ancient Egyptians. Ah yes, the ancients of Egypt are well known for a lot of things. Pyramids, mummies, super cool golden sarcophaguses & booby-trap storylines in many a mid-80s blockbuster Hollywood film.

What you might not know about the ancient Egyptians is that they're believed to be the first people to use OOO as a way of getting messages to the public messages in masse. Yaaaaaaaay, back in 2000 BC, Egyptians started carving out public notices in steel. That's pretty hardcore—imagine something like that happening now! You'd have to quadruple-check there were no last-minute changes before going live.
Can you imagine "pulling" an ad made of steel due to a merch issue or a spelling mistake? YIKES.

Luckily for us, we have brilliant new mediums for advertising to hordes of public. The evolution from steel to digital has taken many turns along its way to get to where we are now. And what a wild ride it has been! The first print ad recorded ran in England in 1472. 1472!!! Since then, we've used print in a million different ways to try & coax readers with the sweetness of our sales pitches. From newspapers to magazines, brochures to flyers, print marketing has a magical quality that most other media don't.

For the most part, printed ads are *portable.* Carrying a brand's message to its ideal end user & then allowing the end user to carry the message even further (literally) seems a fairly smart strategy. Yee haw for portability. Back in the time of the American Revolutionary War, print fliers were distributed in hopes of getting young men to fight.

After the onset (& intervening onslaught of automobiles) & the construction of super-highways in the USA spanning from sea to shining sea, billboards became a great form of marketing to folks hitting the roads. And if you thought digital banner ads were the most innovative thing since innovation was a thing, let us nod to the birth of electric banner ads following the invention of the light bulbs!

Times Square's first electric banner ad went up waaaaaay back in 1882! From 1882 to now, we've seen an explosion of new platforms, technologies, & communication media. With each new innovation came a marketer or ad man (yes, they were almost all men until about 30 years ago) who tried their damndest to fit marketing & advertising into new platforms. From telegraph to radio to television & beyond... we're inundated.

But it's print, the portable & firmly-in-your hands medium, that still carries with it a trust that newer platforms still haven't cultivated with end users. Whether you share your brand in high-end glossy mags or in a weekly newspaper, studies show that—even today—consumers trust print advertising more than digital. Maybe it's in the effort to output. Perhaps it's in the time people have available when sitting down to read a publication. Potentially, it's an amalgamation of both of these factors & even more. Regardless, there's brilliance in print. If you can, explore it!

Radio Advertising

When my brother & I were about 6yrs & 8yrs old, respectively, we used to join our dad at his construction sites for the weekend. Dad built big housing tracts—hundreds of homes at once—which meant he was away most weeks while Rob & I were at school. Dad had the week to build new communities from the ground up while Mom held down the fort & grew us kids. Mom had the weekend for a bit of peace & quiet. I bet she needed it, too!

Anyhow, when we'd go stay with Dad for the weekend on his worksites, we stayed in an old Airstream-esque trailer. There was no TV, no Nintendo, no CDs. All we had was a relic of a transistor radio that spit & spluttered a lot of white noise at us while Dad searched for small moments of rock 'n roll connections. One station camn as clear as day each night: a radio talk show. Lucky for us, the boring adults stopped broadcasting from 8pm–11pm & instead the radio station played radio mysteries & episodic stories from the 1930s & 1940s.

While other kids were getting Mickey Mouse & Saved by The Bell, Rob & I were introduced to the likes of Falcon, The Adventures of Sam Spade, Gunsmoke, & The Glenn Miller Show. Radio shows were magical, transformative, & each night we couldn't wait to get tucked up into bed to find out what would happen next with our favourite characters & storylines. While we easily lost ourselves in the stories, in visualizing everything from the Wild Wild West to detectives in crinkly trench-coats, it was the old-time advertisements that truly excited us. No matter the product or the brand, it was weirdly exciting to listen to the ads when they came on.

Over the modern airwaves, we could hear the crackle and pop of the wrinkles in time that had passed. It was almost as if, each night, the three of us hopped into a time machine and stepped into a world that had been, but that we had never known. The radio ads were stories. They were fantastical and they were imaginative. Each ad, no matter the product had all the elements of sound magic. They would be voice, music, & narratives that left you wanting to know more about the product that most likely didn't even exist any longer. I think it was right there in a little trailer in Rialto, California, that I fell in love with the idea of marketing.

Long before my dad, my brother, & I settled in under the covers in that small trailer, listening to radio ads that were already 50 years old, others had discovered the power of sound in advertising. In fact, way back in 750 BC, the ancient Greeks discovered sonic logos and used them to build burgeoning businesses of love. That's right it was the ladies of the night who put nails into their shoes to produce irresistible come-hither sounds. (Fun fact: Beyond the nails in shoes technique it's also been noted that carved penises pointed towards brothels as well. But I digress.) I mean, think about how brilliant that is for a minute. At some point, some human in the days before modern technology, or any technology, thought, "I need to differentiate myself from all of the other businesses that are open at night." And they came up with an auditory signal to market their wares. Women have always been brilliant marketers. Ohhh la la!

When it comes to modern radio advertising (modern meaning the last 100 years or so), the magical radio advertising I mentioned above started in earnest in the 1920s, when commercial radio stations lanched in the United States. Radio itself was an absolute game changer. When it came to mass reach & the ability to share ideas and communications with entire nations, the power inherent in this channel became a marketer's dream, overnight.

Not only did the medium have scale & the depth, it made space for fantasy & narrative. In a time when many people in the United States & across the world still couldn't read or write, the radio offered an alternative that made communication equitable for all.

Today, radio is still a relevant marketing and advertising platform for expanding the reach of a sponsored event, new product, or interactive cross-channel idea. I personally work in media across all forms of traditional advertising, and it's in the radio side of the business that you still find the most passionate experts. Some might call them egotistical assholes, but really, I say they're just super-duper in love with the magic of the medium they work in.

Radio has completely expanded beyond your basic donut ad breaks, bumper ads, & ad libs live on air. Radio is now not only a trusted platform, but a fully integrated one in the sense that you get a taste of humanity, hilarity, clever storytelling, & the ability to connect to other media, like social media that allows people on the other end of a livestream the ability to participate live & in-person from the comfort of their homes.

Beyond your stereotypical FM and AM stations, we now have a plethora of podcasts, audiobooks, & other audio platforms that act as marketing & sponsorship vehicles. The smartest marketers amongst us still look back to the 40s & the 50s, building modern stories upon traditional foundations that we perfected in an auditory medium so very long ago. Consumers are very smart these days; they don't want to be sold to outright. If you're able to leverage the medium, tell a story, & infuse an auditory ad with cleverness, you're already ahead of the game.

TV & Me
Have you ever gone for a walk outside after dark & noticed the glowing lights illuminating the homes you walk past & the streets around you? Not too long ago, the glowing lights would've been the actual gas lamps or streetlights that're triggered to come on as dusk descends. But recently, when I walk after dark, I am almost always taken aback by how strong the lights are that emanate from television sets.

Whatever you call it—the boob tube, the TV, or the squawk box —there's no escaping its high-definition pull. I've got friends & family members who, when they have new babies, try so hard to keep their kids away from screens—especially television screens. It's as if they fear the television. It's as if they think their kids will lose not only their innocence, but their empathy, their creativity, & their ability to see the world for what it is if they get lost in cartoons or in the metal din of the nightly news. As a mother myself, I've never felt like this. Hell, I'd be an outright asshat of a liar if I said my TV never doubled as a babysitter while I cooked dinner or made time to do adult stuff as my child sat quietly, lost in a cartoon or twenty. That said, this isn't a parenting book, so let's rock right into TV & advertising instead of stirring up a wee shitstorm of opinionated parents.

I remember my mom and dad telling stories about growing up in the 1950s & about the part TV played in their lives as small children. When they were very young, there was only one or two channels & the content streaming through to the TV wasn't 24/7/365 like it is now. For the most part, TV viewing was viewing by appointment. Each week, there were a few shows that were suitable for the entire family.

Just as families did with the radio in earlier times, they gathered around the TV to watch shows that featured stars of the day: mostly people who were talented across the board. Singers, dancers, actors, presenters. They came into family homes each week & brought culture at scale to the USA & other developing nations. My mom has told me stories of watching Hee-Haw every week. She remembers seeing Elvis on TV, as well as The Beatles. She also can pinpoint the exact moment (a wee bit later in her life) when John F. Kennedy was murdered. All of these cultural phenomena played out on the boob tube. A black & white one, at that.

For the last 30 years or so, the TV, and the millions of hours of content created for it, has helped to raise countless children and helped to shape countless cultures. The ways in which we self-identify and the ways in which we move throughout the world are, quite often, dictated by what we see on the small screen. Be it news, culture, sitcoms, drama, violence, sex, or happy cartoon rainbow fairies, we are all a part of the TV game.

It only stands to reason, then, that TV advertising would be the one channel to rule them all. TV ads originated in the 1940s in earnest, promoting political campaigns—LOL, oh the irony. I've dug pretty deep to try and find some of the oldest TV ads known, & the most fascinating piece of the puzzle when it comes to TV advertising is also the piece that makes the most sense. As with any media platform, the oldest TV ads were static images with radio voiceovers. Without knowing how to use the platform to its full potential, early advertisers took what they knew (which was radio advertising) & applied these roles to a new medium.

TV didn't stay static for long. Beginning in the 1950s and 1960s, advertising began building some of the biggest brands that still exist today. A mixture of moving pictures and musical mastery meant that advertising didn't feel like selling. I grew up in the heyday of television advertising in the 1980s and 1990s. At this point in time, television advertising had reached peak maturity level. To this day, I can still close my eyes and see Juicy Fruit gum commercials, sing the Toys-R-Us jingle, and tell you just how grrrrrrreat Frosted Flakes are, thanks to Tony the Tiger.

In fact, looking back on at all, our little brains sure were filled to the brim with the promise of tasty, sugar laden sensations that doubled as breakfast food. Remember being cuckoo for Coco Pops? Or even when Sugar Pops changed their name to Corn Pops in an attempt to trick moms and dads into buying little yellow globlits of sugary amazingness? Yeah, I can remember all of that, & I also remember the product placement in cartoons. In everything from Rainbow Brite to The Care Bears, to the Smurfs & G.I. Joe, there was always a hard sell that didn't feel anything more than a gentle nudge when you're little.

Looking back, I can see why we needed so many regulations around advertising the kids. Talk about a wide-open wasteland of advertising wonderment. On the other side, we had a lot of educational advertising around programs like DARE. These advertorials took hard-line stances when it came to alcohol & drug use.

Most people my age can remember in startling detail the anti-drug television commercial in which eggs are broken into a frying pan. A hard voiceover says, "This is your brain," whilst showing unbroken eggs. The dramatic scene is resolved by cracking the eggs into a sizzling, oiled pan with the voiceover warning, "This is your brain on drugs!" I don't know about you, but I did not want my brain to sizzle like Friday eggs in a hot pan.

Because of its reach, scale, & ability to hook consumers through strong storytelling, TV advertising became the strongest form of advertising available to brands, & the most expensive. It still blows my mind that advertisers & agencies push TV as the number-one way of reaching & affecting consumers. Most traditional ad agencies still build campaigns from TV out, instead of consumer first.

Humans digest their visual content differently now. Most people subscribe to services like Netflix or Hulu, or other local options, yet traditional, terrestrial television is still the go-to for advertising bods.

While I don't doubt the importance of TV in a modern marketing mix, I don't think that TV is the be-all & end-all anymore. I get it: traditional media equals a great playground for the ego. People that we see on TV, movies, or on the news are still heralded as important people to be celebrated. Which means that mini-Siennas & brand marketers think TV is the best method for gaining brand frame.

It's up to us, the modern marketers of today, to give a damn when it comes to building better advertising. Sure, a flashy TV ad campaign can still sometimes cut through the din. But unless you're able to take that TV campaign & build other ways of connecting with others & building conversations that extend from the boob-tube itself (such as digital and social media platforms), you might just be a little bit hamstrung. Where once the brilliant TV advertisers of yesteryear were the visionaries of their time, the evolution of marketing beyond TV now seems merely inevitable. This leads us to the new frontier; which, if we're honest with ourselves, isn't really all that new.

Internet Advertising

With the onset of personal home computers & the pervasiveness of technology in every part of our modern lives, it's hard to imagine a media landscape without Internet advertising. From ad blockers to banner blindness, we are all old hat at the game of Internet advertising. But it hasn't always been that way. In fact, when we look back, Internet advertising only really took root at scale in the mid-1990s. This was the time of banner ads. The main space invaders at the beginning were, of course, telecommunications companies & their agencies. Makes sense, doesn't it?

Telecommunications agencies are businesses that survive on connecting us, so marketing to us through the media they served and built made perfect sense. In the late 90s (1997, to be exact), the first mobile advertisement was sent loose into the world, thanks to a Finnish news service that started sharing their headlines via SMS. If you're my age or older, & can remember life before the Internet, there was an absolute cool factor in getting mobile advertisements when they were brand-new.

But the sheen & the shine sure wore off quickly when marketers got greedy & started to invade our most private means of communication: our phones. There's always been a line that marketers & advertisers must tread carefully.

But since the advent of Internet & mobile technology, marketers have really stepped over that line.

Stepping over the line; rather, long-jumping past it, started in earnest during the 2000s. We had it all, didn't we? Banner ads, pop-up ads, interstitial ads... We had all the goddamn ads. It felt gross then, & it still feels gross now. With this clear shift away from storytelling towards seemingly targeted & personalized advertising, we lost our privacy & became data points to big businesses hell-bent on selling to us.

For a long time, brands forgot that at the end of the data point and behind the blue dot on a Google map resided a human being with hopes, dreams, & desires that drove their purchase behavior—not last-click attribution models.

When we started out in the digital realm, we were standing on the shoulders of extraordinary advertising legends. We were also, unknowingly, waving goodbye to the equity they felt in their own careers & in their own artistry, & welcoming in the new era of democratized reach, influence, & feedback. The game changers amongst us aren't always visionaries. They are people who find hidden value in things that others consistently overlook. Most of the time, this hidden value isn't hidden at all. In fact, it's out there in plain sight for all to see. We need only to look beyond our own little bubbles & raise our eyes to the level of real life. To succeed in Internet-digital-social-media-whatever-you-want-to-call-it advertising, you must remember the human at the other end of your advertisement first, not last.

Social Media is Dead – Long Live Social Media

Beep bop boop... Welcome to the era of social media. It's 2019 right now, which means social media has only been around in earnest for about 13 years. But I wonder if any of us can remember a world without social media? I mean really remember it. For me, life before social media was strangely fuller. I had a small group of very good friends, a strong center of gravity that was my nuclear family, & a few heroes and legends I grew up wanting to become. I remember when I first got my Hotmail account. A free email service! I used said Email service to send messages to my friends while we chatted on the old-fashioned landline telephone.

In the beginning, Internet communities were built on already existing ones, which is why, I believe, the heralding and of social media was celebratory & mostly positive. Fast forward to today, & most people would agree that social media brings out the worst in humanity more often than it brings out the best. All you need to do was look in the comments sections of divisive & inflammatory headlines to find a raging cesspool of negative and hurtful humanity.

Around about the time that marketers, advertisers, & brands cottoned on to the fact that social media wasn't going away anytime soon, we started to become an advertiser's dream & humanity's worst nightmare.

I can remember coming of age professionally in this time. Hands up if you, too, were looked at like part soothsayer, part crazy-professor, & part unicorn-wrangler back when social media first became a "thing" that businesses got a sniff of as a powerful tool for reaching people (if your hand is up, you are one of my people).

This was a time when going to work every day meant busting my butt to earn a very small wage. This was a time when being a social media &/or digital marketer was akin to unproven magic. For almost a decade, there wasn't a single day that went by in which traditional marketers & TV advertisers would look at me with sad eyes, giggle while they headed out to long agency lunches, & call out to me, "Social media girl, enjoy your community building." As if community building & understanding new digital landscapes were things for me to be ashamed of.

From the beginning of social media for brands, a few very astute contemporaries & I warned brands about the adverse side-effects of marketing in spaces that weren't built to be bulldozed into. We counselled our marketing elders & begged them not to burn all of the trust we'd built by shouting, to begging for sales, & putting up shit content in places where marketers were not welcome.

Not many people listened; instead, they were dazzled by shallow promises & driven by ROI that was never really proven by any singular channel. Success metrics were driven by money making, not by making communities stronger. Reach, volume, clicks. Reach, volume, clicks. Rinse & repeat, until no one trusts brands or platforms anymore.

That's the dark hole we're all finding ourselves at the bottom of—looking up towards a clear blue sky, asking consumers to throw us a rope. Throw into the mix influencer marketing & we're stretched so damn thin. Our contemporaries are still lost in believing that hacking algorithms will somehow mean we hack humanity. Social media marketing has become beige lately, & we've only ourselves to blame.

Remember those five years when large agencies kept promising "viral videos" for the right price? Yeah, it was gross then & it's gross now to promise likeability based on purchase & over-inflated viewership rates. While we're lost in trying to outspend & out-perform our rivals in the arena of media buying, our favourite consumers are quickly falling out of love with us.

So how do we find magic again? How do we put consumers first whilst growing our bottom lines? There are endless ways; we simply need to stop for a moment. We need to stop spinning our wheels & start adding value back into the lives of our customers. To do this, we need to understand not just the platforms we're using, & not just the history of these platforms—we need to know *why* we exist.

Do you know, off the top of your head, the reason why your business is a business at all? What do you do to make this world a better place? What kinds of stories can you unearth to connect people positively? Can you imagine a marketing plan where you spend nothing—not a single red cent—on social media, but instead, invest it into customer experience? When you can work through all of these questions & clearly answer them in a short elevator pitch that doesn't end in, "and then our revenue grew to XXX," then you'll be on the right path forward into a world that is embracing circular economies, sustainability, & longevity based on moral compass.

To be a great marketer, you need only a pinch of common sense, a lust for life, & a passion for making the world a better place. From there, the rest is storytelling & efficiency in operations. Go get it!

CAN MARKETING SAVE US?

Tina Turner may not need another hero, but let's face it: most of us do. We're not all badass booty-shaking queens filled with endless energy, wily femininity, & rock 'n roll, like she is. We need our heroes. We long for them. And when we cannot see them right in front of us, we invent them for comfort's sake. From the dawning of days, humans have looked & longed for a savoir. Whether saving ourselves, saving others, or saving the planet, marketing has been tasked with driving some pretty heady changes over the millennia.

More than simply peddling consumable wares & services, our superpowers as storytellers, salespeople, leaders, & creative gymnasts of colloquial slang have been tapped into, as if we possess some sort of black magic of persuasion or gris gris of go-getter-ness. There's reason for this, too. Creative people offer new solutions to old problems Persuasive people lead. Leaders inspire change. And, though we fear it more than anything, it is change that could save us all. Yadda yadda yadda... you get what I'm saying.

But can marketing *actually save us?* I sure hope so, because (let's not be naïve here) it's marketing that has gotten us into a whole heap of trouble. The cynic in me looks at where we are today when it comes to our home: Planet Earth. Mother Nature is heating up. Her ice-caps are melting at alarming rates. Science be damned, there are folks who think that because it snows in Detroit in the middle of winter that the rest of the earth isn't limping after decades of humanity running amok with our atmosphere. But no honey, no. Look at your hands. I'll look at mine.

For decades, we've been pumping our land, seas, & air full of pollution. We've been the biggest throw-away generation ever. One day, posterity will look back & think HOW THE HELL DID THEY NOT KNOW ABOUT THE _____ (PLASTIC/FOSSIL FUELS/INSERT BAD IDEA THAT SEEMED GOOD AT SCALE HERE)?!?

Many of us are already coming to terms with childhoods that included using & then tossing away a mountain of single-use plastic & Styrofoam. It's as if we didn't know any better. How did we not know any better? I can clearly remember Christmas mornings. Unwrapping toys, only to then endure an impatient (& seemingly endless) struggle with layer upon layer of plastic packaging. Do you remember this? Everything was wrapped, covered, encased, entombed in plastic so thick that normal kitchen scissors wouldn't suffice.

It took military-grade machetes or the Jaws of Life to extricate GI Joe or your Nintendo game from its temporary home. Temporary. We used to take all that packaging & just toss it into the trash can. All of it. Without one single thought. WHAT THE ACTUAL FUCK.

In all reality, marketing told us this behaviour was okay. In fact, this behaviour was normal. It was normal to not give a single damn about the impact we were having on the planet. Our job was to drive consumer societies. It was up to us to keep the coal fires burning (literally) & to save the world by solidifying our way of life. Keeping up with the Joneses strangled our planet. It's only now that we're understanding how wounded our planet is. I could weep for Mother Earth.

So, if marketing is what drove us to buy, buy, buy & use, use, use, how do we use the same power to clean up the mess & make sure things like this don't happen again? First, we need to check our egos & our long-entrenched processes at the proverbial (& the literal) door. Saving the planet might not look so good to your company's bottom line—but economic factors as indicators of a successful business are myopic, singular, & short term. Money talks, but consciousness walks.

Heal The World; Make it a Better Place
As businesses & the people who run them become more woke, we're seeing a big shift back towards being purposeful in how we conduct money making. The term *environmentally friendly* has been around since time immemorial (if not that long, it's been here since the 1980s at least), but *being* environmentally friendly & sustainable hasn't been a way in which most business comport themselves for a long, long time. Luckily, as we of the gross consumable generation come of age, we're also insisting that business does the same.

Take IKEA, for example. Recently, they have invested in sustainability & a circular economy model throughout their entire business operations system. From supply chain through to waste reduction & beyond, IKEA is working towards better for all—including the earth & humanity.

Patagonia, a Californian company with major cool-factor, has been leaning super-hard into corporate social responsibility for a long time now. In fact, in a decidedly tongue-in-cheek nod to crusading against superfluous & conspicuous consumption, Patagonia's business & marketing model is one that promotes "anti-growth." Patagonia also has put their money where their proverbial mouth is: taking political stands & advocating for governmental policy globally that drives sustainable business practices. Wait, WHAAAAAAAAT?! A company with heart. Be still mine.

Thanks to brands that are becoming enlightened again, marketers now have stories to tell that matter. We can do things that are bigger than ourselves. But with great power comes great responsibility. If we comport ourselves as professionals with ethical, responsible, sincere, sustainable & long-term visions of a cleaner planet, how do we bring others along for the ride? Well, as I see it, the solution is as complex as it is simple: we now have a new normal to embed across the board.

We all must play our part.

Beyond corporations playing their parts collectively, advertising big-wigs have been flexing their muscles for a while now when it comes to changing the world. Have you ever heard of *Earth Day?* It started waaaaaaaaaaaaaaaay back in 1970. Millions of people took part (dude, MILLIONS!) in the first Earth Day, & it is now recognised globally as the largest movement focused on taking action to driving political change around the impact of industrial harm on our planet. It's estimated that over ONE BILLION people in 192 countries now recognise Earth Day annually. Holy Toledo, Batman! That's a heckuva lot of people marking a moment to think about their impact on our one & only planet. And it's all thanks to Julian Koenig. Well, kinda.

You see, Koenig wasn't a scientist or a professional political activist. On the other end of the planet-saving spectrum, he was & is still considered one of the greatest copywriters in the history of advertising. Remember those Timex ads, "It takes a licking and keeps on ticking"? The VW "Think Small" ads? Yep, those are Mr K.'s handiwork. But, clever as they were, neither of those campaigns were ever going to help save the planet.

Enter Earth Day.

Before Earth Day was Earth Day, it was a small movement that lacked formidable followership. Organisers originally wanted Earth Day to be an environmental teach-in. They were fairly stumped for a catchy name for the event, though. Thus, Koenig stepped in & added a little spark of genius to the event that would last until this very day. He came up with a series of names for the movement (the event was always going to become a movement), & in coming up with names such as Earth Day, Ecology Day, Environment Day, & E Day, he added urgency, flair, & a collective ability to scale the event through language. He also made it very clear that the team would be, erm, idiots if they didn't choose Earth Day as the name of their event.

Also of note: Earth Day sounds like *birthday*—April 22nd happens to be both Earth Day & Koenig's birthday. When I sit & think about something as simple as a brilliant copywriter's contribution to a movement that might've petered out before it had even begun, I'm heartened knowing that advertising & marketing can really help to shape the world we all inhabit. With strong marketing & a strong purpose at its core, Earth Day still oozes with genuine authenticity both globally & locally. Talk about guts & heart.

What's next for us? What can we all turn our hands to when it comes to helping leave the planet a better, healthier place than we found it? I would like to put a thought out into the world right now—a planting of a seed, of sorts: every day, in every way, it is now on you, Dear Reader, to help. It is up to you to use your superpowers not simply to drive consumption & grow an already fat bottom line, but to give back. To grow others. To embed a more circular view of how we live. May we leave more of a mark by literally leaving less of one.

Beyond Earth Day, retail giants like IKEA are starting to make change happen by actually changing things (weird strategy, I know, doing stuff in order to get stuff done). Recently IKEA started growing produce (mainly lettuce) in shipping containers outside of selected stores in Sweden. Goddamn it, I love Sweden so much—almost as much as I love salad! Seriously, though, if you know anyone from Southern California, you'll know our passion for all things lettuce, kale, & saladesque.

When asked about why the company is investing in growing their own lettuce & other scrummy yummy veges, IKEA answered pretty simply, stating that, "Urban farming has the potential to transform the global food value chain, as it aims to produce local fresh food within close proximity to meet demand, all while using less natural resources." Long story short, it costs a lot of money to make salads when you have to import all of the ingredients mostly year-round. Who knew the carbon footprint on a head of lettuce could be nearly debilitating?

So how's IKEA growing their urban farming goods? Pretty simple, really. Inside of each shipping container, a hydroponic growing system holds four levels of plants. This is the equivalent of (up to) 3,600 heads of lettuce. YASSSS SALADS I SEE YOU, even in Swedish winters. To make matters even better, there's no soil, pesticides, or herbicides needed to grow special IKEA shipping container goodies. The system uses up to 90% less water than growing crops in a field which I, as a sample size of one whilst tippity typing away growing hungrier for a hearty Cobb, see as probably the best thing since sliced bread. LED lights that are powered by renewable energy sources—like the rest of the Ikea stores—are used to assist the plants in growing as quickly as possible. The lettuce also gets nutrients from food waste. Talk about WIN-WIN-WIN.

To continue my fangirling of IKEA for a hot moment, it's important to note that food & consumables are a relatively small part of the company's overall carbon footprint. That said, the company is committed to sustainability being an interwoven, strategic aspect across the company. Like other businesses focused on more than short-term gain at the expense of the earth & humanity, IKEA's look towards creating a circular model of consumption (they're already experimenting with renting the furniture in their stables) means that food must be a piece of the solution.

Why? Well, globally, more than 30% of climate emissions are connected to food. 30%! We all have to eat, so I get it. But wow, we're really going to need to step up our efforts at scale to grow & consume locally. Especially as the human race continues to grow. I'd love to see more businesses aim for "climate positive" (meaning that it reduces more emissions than it creates) operating models. Until then, we have lessons in lettuce to impassion us & feed our souls & bodies at once.

IKEA, world saver. And salad champion of the Swedes?

Girl, You'll Be A (Pretty) Woman Soon
When it comes to saving our planet, businesses & brands aren't allowed to be passive anymore. The harm inflicted on our planet in the past century alone by industry & consumer business is enough for all of us to insist that marketing & business start putting their money where it counts. Marketing, I reckon, can & will help to save the planet. But will it help to save our souls?

Growing up in Southern California, I was always a bit more Jodie Foster than I was Pamela Anderson. I grew up rough & ready & completely at home playing sports from sunup to sundown. My younger brother Rob (we're only 16 months apart) & I were always together. Our friendship groups melded together early on, too. We lived a life where boys & girls & sports & music & everything stereotypically girlish or boyish was blurred. For a burning hot minute (a.k.a. decade), I was a confident little girl who really believed that she could take on the world & win.

However, that all changed as I came of age. As a millennial at the older end of the spectrum, I remember a bit of childhood without devices, but never a time without games, screens, & connections to others. As I came into my more formative years & started to take into account the space I took up in the world —that which I wanted to take up & that which I was allowed to take up—changed. It happened slowly, but all at once. I went to school & got good grades. I had a strong group of friends: we all played sports together & were Girl Scouts.

I consumed content that swirled all around me non-stop. There was *Saved By the Bell*, *Tiger Beat* magazine, billboards of Cindy Crawford lining city streets. So-Cal, eh? Land of dreams, rainbows, butterflies, & a very pointed view of what both femininity & masculinity should look like.

I was taught by advertising that I needed to be *less* of something. I couldn't put my finger on exactly what I should be *less* of, so I became *less* of me. I did what most teenage girls from Southern California (or anywhere, for that matter, who have access to shitty-ass media platforms that propagate a certain idea of how ALL WOMEN should present themselves): I became smaller. Blonder. More tanned. Less confident in my strength. Less confident in myself. More concerned about what others thought when they looked at me. I got myself very deep down a dark hole of over-exercising & not eating enough. I stopped looking in the mirror.

As hard as it is to write this, marketing & advertising stole my best years from me, really. All of the bullshit in *Teen Vogue* that taught me to take up less space & to allow more for men secretly had me questioning everything my parents had taught me. They taught me to stand strong, to work hard, to fight for what's right, & to use my voice to help others. Hell, I couldn't even help myself.

Fast forward 20 years & many therapy sessions later... and here I am, clawing back to confidence. As a mother of a teenage daughter, I am very aware of the marketing & advertising she's consuming. We talk about it often. We play "spot the Photoshopped image." We talk about how important it is not to buy into the fact that even the most affordable & accessible retailers have marketers who still bend the knee to merch teams who only allow size 8 models in sales catalogues—even when their key audiences are, on average, a size 14-16. WTAF?

Mostly, though, my daughter & I talk about how eschewing culturally accepted norms of femininity & masculinity isn't easy. Our teen suicide rates are ridiculously, heartbreakingly high. We cannot go on like this as a global society. Our children do not need to endure torture when it unceasingly comes to them in the form of smiling perfection that is created in a studio. How do we unpack centuries of defining "normal" & awaken to the people around us as they are? How do we throw "normal" away & simply allow people to be? I'm not sure if a single big step is the best way to approach change, or if a million small ones might be better. All I know is that things need to change.

Numerous studies over the past few decades have told us with 100% certainty that people judge themselves based on what they see in the media. We're also facing a time when most models we see weigh an average of 23% less than a typical woman. Just twenty years ago, this difference was a mere 8%.
Why the change? Well, as it turns out, over twenty years ago, the diet business was not as profitable as it is now, with much of this relating to the media. Today, this industry consists of over $33 billion each year. Also playing into all of this is the fact that women are continually portrayed as sexualized objects: vehicles to sell cheeseburgers, cars, window cleaner, you name it. Alongside this toxic marketing is a 400% rise in instances of eating disorders between 1970 & today. FOUR HUNDRED GODDAMN PERCENT. Bleurgh. I think I just vomited in my mouth a little bit.

We can do better as an industry.
We must do better as an industry.
We must not fear changing the world for the better & healthier.

Here's an interesting look backwards for all of us. I recently read an article about beauty standards—how they have & haven't really changed all that much over time. For example, in 1957, hair colouring was a taboo subject. TABOO! Can you imagine? As a modern woman who doles out a small fortune annually to keep my blonde locks unencumbered by encroaching greys & mousey brown roots, I can only imagine the time & money I'd save if it wasn't for Miss Clairol in 1957. A tagline of the day posed the question, "does she or doesn't she?", wondering whether or not your BFF or your naughty neighbour coloured her hair. I mean, talk about bloody nosy. But marketing, as always & forever attempting to hack society & change it for the sake of driving sales, birthed new beauty standards.

When the Miss Clairol ad dropped, the odds were 15:1 that the answer was "no." But within 10 years, the odds went to 2:1. An industry & a new era were born, and unrealistic beauty standards were injected into our already wobbly, media-driven psyches. Not only did we need to dress for, lose weight for, be proper for our men... now we needed to colour our goddamn hair. *eyes roll out of head*

Fast forward 60 years & we've got Dove & other big-money brands positioning themselves at the center of beauty & self-confidence. Dove's "Real Beauty sketches" brought to light how we, as women, see ourselves by asking a number of women to describe themselves to a sketch artist. After describing themselves, these same women were asked to describe each other to the same artist. Each participant started the campaign experiment as strangers, & the results were shockingly not shocking.

What bubbled to the top were both common narratives & hard

truths. When describing themselves, each participant high-lighted their own perceived flaws. The sketches they were returned from the artist looked nothing like them. Whereas the sketches drawn when strangers described each other looked more truthful—more inherently individual & beautiful. When Dove dropped their campaign video, more than 50 million people viewed it within the first 12 days of its release.

I'm not going to lie: since becoming a mom, I am an easy target for tear-inducing storytelling. Hell, I'll come clean here & tell you that I've been known to cry when EVERYBODY GETS A CAR from Oprah. This Dove campaign, though, it punched me right in the gut & in the feels. Dove's takeaway lesson of "*(Beauty) could be as easy as seeing ourselves through a stranger's eyes*" was a wake-up call for marketers & everyday humans equally. With a singular storytelling campaign device, Dove out-clevered an all-too-clever industry. Whether or not you buy into the lesson of a simple campaign, we must do better by our women & girls. And, by rights, our young men too.

I have a few ideas on *HOW* we can lead conversations & change how society sees the importance & power of individuality.

STEPS TO DO BETTER

Stand. The. Fuck. Up.
Seriously. Stand. The. Fuck. Up.
The days of brands sitting back & being faceless entities are dead & buried. Without a purpose, without a rallying cry, & without a morality that is easily discernible as your North Star, you're nothing. Humans need stories to understand a business, a person, a process, a product. If you don't know your story, people won't care. Big businesses in particular have the power to change the world. Seriously, imagine if BIG businesses stopped spending even a single red cent on the main social media platforms. They'd peter out faster than a fast thing. Facebook, Instagram, Google, YouTube, Twitter... they all know

this! That's why they woo CEOs, CMOs, & CDOs, & play to fallible human egos. Because that's where the power & the money are. Without the money machines behind them, social channels become—GASP—social. Instead of being delivery machines for ads of which 99% are irrelevant & will never matter to a single human, they would have to pivot. To change. To weed out the Bad Actors.

As it is, with all of the under-the-table handshakes, trips to sunny climes, & "secret projects" that make big people feel BIG-GER... nothing will change until a few truly influential people stop the machine by growing a proverbial pair (LUSH UK!). I love the Good Actors, though. The brands that wear their hearts & their commitments to people & the planet on their sleeves. Literally. My mind goes to Patagonia & $10m in tax breaks—erm, rather, donations that they gave back after seeing just how ridiculous a tax cut is on a company that earns a whole lotta dosh.

Then you've got smaller labels, like Wildfang & their "We Care, Don't You?" stand taken after Melania Trump's infamous gaffe during a time when children were being systematically taken from their families at the United States border. By putting their money & their product where their heart is, Wildfang is another Brand Boo of mine. They just don't put a foot wrong, & that's not due to stepping lightly, either. They stand the fuck up. Often. We need more brands like Patagonia & Wildfang.

Call out the bullshit when you see it.
Don't play the *Size 8 Game*. More importantly, refuse to be a part of it by not purchasing from businesses that proliferate damaging societal stereotypes around gender, size, health, creed, or colour. Fuck the buyers & the merch teams who only give you size 6 & size 8 samples. We're marketers, Team: we can DEMAND clothes that fit 95% of the population. We can tell better stories visually. And we can create powerful ads that feature real

people. Believe it or not, over 39% of marketing professionals report some kind of mental health or stress-related issue. We're the insiders, we know the game. Just imagine how hard navigating the world must feel for people who don't realise we're able to rewrite the damn rules. It's up to us on the front lines to call out bullshit when we see it. Not to simply be noticed, but to help redefine self-care, self-love, & self-appreciation.

Stop propagating trends that encourage negative behaviours

Weight loss supplements—bullshit.
Pills to make your skin smoother—bullshit.
Juice detoxes—bullshit.
No cellulite—bullshit.

So many trends are complete & utter crap. They live & die on us not feeling good about ourselves. We, as marketers, we have the absolute power to do & be better by & for humanity. Everything we put out into the world must have some sort of moral compass attached to it—even if that moral compass is a slight change. A wee tickle in the back of your mind that reminds you that your impact reaches further than an impression on a website or a view of an article. Let's plan & build our campaigns around positive impact & leave the negativity somewhere far, far, far in the past.

Can marketing save us from ourselves?
Yeah, I think it can.

But it starts with me & you. Are you in?

CAREER-LIMITING

As humans, we're judgmental. It's in our nature. No matter how much meditation we commit ourselves to, or how self-aware we are, there's always a small seed of something that reminds us of our otherness, regardless of how similar we are when everything's boiled down to intention, love, & kindness.

While I get super frustrated with the highlighted sense of eat-or-be-eaten in some corporate settings, I get it. I don't like it, & tend to run from workplace cultures that are anything other than accepting of diverse opinions, but I get it. We're all just a few strands of DNA coding away from being a few steps down the evolutionary charts. We're lucky to have evolved as far as we have—but we have a way to go yet.

Back in prehistoric days, being able to quickly assess a situation & decipher whether it was a life or death moment, or whether someone was friend or foe, was how we lived to old enough ages to procreate and—eventually—evolve as a species. Our brain takes a million tiny shortcuts that we usually don't notice. If we had to take the long road to discovery every time we made a decision, our lives would be nothing but big ol' stalemates.

I begin this chapter with a few tidbits of information about how our brains are wired simply to bring us gently into a topic that really gets my knickers in a knot: *Judgemental Asshats & Career Limiting Moves.* As marketers, not only are we fantabulous crafters of succinct messages that drive consumers to consume more, but we are also A1, Gold Star, Judgy McJudgersons.

While you personally might not be chasing your ego's tail on the daily, catty doesn't even begin to cover it. If you think back on your career, I imagine you're a bit like me & can pick out at least half a dozen moments of judgemental assholishness that are seared into your memory for the pain, awe, or weirdness they brought to your life.

As I've become older, I've realized that kindness is often misconstrued as weakness when it comes to playing the advertising game. Also, with the beautiful clarity of hindsight, I see that the same kindness that might signal weakness to others also builds intestinal fortitude like no other. And it helps to build better leaders... but more on that later.

Most things we do as marketers can garner us a fresh gasp or stinky side-eye from our desk jockey colleagues... and I mean most things! One of the moments-in-time that has stuck with me over time (& I imagine always will) was a moment at a past place of employment. This company was trying—rather, the people team was trying—to help their employees achieve a bit more balance at work. The company was big, burgeoning, & burning people out at the seams with overwork.

As a way of giving back & helping to stem the tide of burnout, the business started to offer 30-minute yoga sessions at lunchtime for people who needed a little bit of a pick-me-up on a Wednesday or a Friday. What a fantastic idea! A company that FINALLY GETS IT! Workers are not data points or names written haphazardly on an org chart. Nope, employees are humans who need 30 minutes twice a week to actually step away from their desks, to find quiet, & to re-energize. Cool, right?! Super cool. Let's be honest, too, of 12,000 employees, only about 15 took the business up on this offer, which I thought was a bit of a shame, but hey... 15 people with clearer minds isn't something to shake a branch at.

The classes were well run and everyone seemed to think simply having them in the office was a step forward in building a better culture. Well, not everyone. You guessed it: over the course of a couple of weeks, I overheard a few of my marketing compatriots making snide comments. Everything from the spandex on show, to people not wearing shoes (ferchrissakes, this is GOD-DAMN NAMASTE TWISTY STRETCHY YOGA YOU JUDGEMEN-TAL ASSHOLES!), & more.

I tended to ignore most of the unwarranted & unwanted catty commentary, but a real pearl of a comment came in the form of one woman—high enough up in the organization to know better, but still egotistical enough not to give one ounce of a shit about how base her opinions could sometimes be. As this colleague and I walked between meetings, we passed the meeting room-cum-yoga studio & saw the 15 hearty, calm souls inside, practicing their pretzel-like-stretches.

These humans were beautiful. For all of their curves, stretches, ohms, & downward facing dogs, they were investing in themselves. They were taking our business up on the promise of having even a tiny little snippet of calm in our days that didn't equate to ROI, spreadsheets, or delivery of customer benefits. In just over a nanosecond, my heart swelled in seeing these folks take the time they'd been offered. My reverie state of pride in cool colleagues was soon shattered, through, & I was brought skidding back to reality. Just as I was about to say something in praise of the folks taking the time to do well by themselves (& the business for bringing this to them), my colleague turned to me, pointed to the yoga room, and loudly said, "You see that?"

I nodded.

"THAT is career-limiting."

WHAT FRESH HELL WAS I LIVING IN, TEAM?

We know that we're working too much without turning our minds or our devices off. We're privy to the information, the white papers, the deep dive scientific examinations of our health, & even more so, to a heavy pull that tells us with nary a whisper that we're exhausted. Bone tired. And we need to take time to do something other than to be corporate automatons.

When business-sanctioned, lunchtime yoga becomes something that's career-limiting in the eyes of (most likely, very jealous peers), we have to realize just how fucked-up our culture is. And we need to help fix it.

Beyond yoga, I've noticed quite a few other things that are also looked upon as career-limiting in marketing; but in the actual real world, they're things to be celebrated & held up to a light. The following list is just a tip-toe into the tide of limiting ways of being, but they're a good starting point:

- **Having an opinion**
(especially as a woman and as NTHPPITR—not the highest paid person in the room.)
- **Trying new things**
- **Being too individual**
- **Not being individual enough**
- **Being TOO successful (show me your failures!)**

All in all, the most career-limiting attributes are some of the most enjoyable things in life. Anything done in spandex is frowned upon—though I'd live my life in the stuff if my daughter would be seen in public with me wearing it. I imagine there will come a day when all of my give-a-damns will be busted and activewear will become my every day, every way wear. Deal with it, future world. Deal with it.

Back to today, though, a time in which overt self-betterment can be seen as presumptuous & preachy. Ferchrissakes, Momma just wants a little definition in her arms before bingo-wings happily appear. They're not far off.

Beyond self-care of the physical body, there's mental wellbeing. Starting when we're young marketing pups, we're led to believe that if we're going to fly high, we might just need to burn all of our candles at both ends. As an old hound, I beg of you: please don't do this. All it will do is teach you to intrinsically link your self-worth to a job title.

We're all so much more than words on paper, written by people who didn't know us before we came in for a job interview. Define yourself. Know yourself. And make boundaries that are the written law when it comes to being mentally & spiritually healthy.

In a lot of the organisations I've worked for in the past, our people & support teams have worked their asses off (and spent a lot of time & money) to bring really amazing mental health programmes into the workplace. But if partaking in these pro-grammes is still seen as taboo, then they're rendered nil & void before we're even able to explore them. My advice is simple: lis-ten to your gut, take people up on offers of help when needed, & don't be afraid to open up. If anyone's going to judge you for your beautiful imperfections & deeply-cultivated quirks, they're the sad sacks... not you.

In talking career-limiting, I see folks who can't see past their next tenuous campaign launch as life-limiting. Me? I set firm boundaries on my time, expectations, outputs, & health. Small daily moments of revolution might seem like big hassles at the time, but I can tell you they're the things that others will be watching. Your badass stance on leaving the office & turning off emails when you go is something more of us need to do. What-ever balance looks like to you, embrace it. Own it. Live it.

For all of the things that we should fear to be career-limiting, let's tackle them & break them down to the big stuff. Sweating the small stuff just leaves most people with an inflated sense of being better than others & with nothing to show for their toil over time. Maybe it's ego, but my soul needs a little applause (and rest) after a shit-ton of toil.

SHEEP GO TO HEAVEN

Growing up, my childhood was split between two realities. I lived most of the year in sunny Southern California with my Mom, Dad, & younger brother Rob. Being only 16 months apart, Rob & spent a lot of time at the beach getting happily pummeled by beautifully breaking waves (eventually, we learned how to ride on top of them, but as kids, we were happy frolicking & learning about the literal ebb & flow of life). We also spent a lot of time during the school year—and sometimes during the holidays—playing all kinds of sports. Our California reality was akin to rainbows & butterflies. Looking back, we couldn't have been luckier.

Beyond our California life, though, we spent a lot of time with our family in rural Missouri. Our Mom was raised in a small town of just over 225 people in post-WWII America. And as much as I adored being a beachy So-Cal kid, nothing compared to my time on the farm. Alongside our 10,000 cousins (there were 12 of us, but it felt like 10,000 once you layered in second & third cousins), we explored the woods, learned to shoot arrows, drove John Deere tractors, rode motorcycles, helped Grandpa feed & water the animals, delivered the mail on the local rural route, & drank copious amounts of sweet tea—hot tea in the winter, cold tea in the summer.

As we got older, Rob stopped coming to Missouri for vacations to concentrate on playing sports at high levels. Me? I kept jumping on planes & heading to Grandma & Grandpa's place. As a teenager, I oftentimes found myself alone when staying with my grandparents. By this time, all my cousins were grown up, out actively searching for adventures beyond the farm. Of all my time spent in Missouri growing up, it was this time, as I tip-toed around the idea of transitioning into adulthood, that sticks with me most. This was the time when I had the wisdom of my grandmother & my grandfather all to myself.

Day in & day out, I'd get up before dawn & join Grandpa for his morning chores. Whatever they were, we did them together. Of all the things I remember about my Grandpa, it's his patience that stays with me. And his hands. As he aged, he moved more slowly. I can recall with utmost clarity his hands as he tied his black leather shoes with such intention. Routine was surely a part of how he went about getting ready to face another day, but if he did anything in his life, I knew for a fact he did it intentionally.

My grandma was much the same. She would wake early to fix each of us a hot cup of tea. I can remember how she boiled the jug, warmed the teapot, & then allowed the tea to brew under a handmade tea cozy. She, too, was intentional in all things she said & did. I miss both of these humans so much my heart could just burst.

But there will be no bursting hearts right now! The intention of telling you about two differing facets of a life that shaped who I am now is because, from the very beginning of my life, I knew for a fact that one person could survive & thrive in more than one "home." I also knew that being intentional with what you say, do, & bring into the world was a way in which I would personally like to comport myself throughout my precious time on this spinning rock in the middle of space.

It only makes sense that, when I chose to move to New Zealand at 21 yrs old, that I'd be moving to a country that was very much an amalgamation of the City Mouse/Country Mouse lifestyle I grew up with. Auckland itself is a big, bustling hub of activity—but head 20 minutes out of the city in any direction, & you will find yourself in a rolling countryside that very much looks like Missouri in Spring or Autumn. It took me but a nanosecond to fall in love with my new country, & falling in love with the people of NZ happened even faster.

When I think about going through life intentionally, making the decision to move far from home, starting a family in a new country, & jumping into a career that I knew would offer a plethora of ways for me to dive into my creative skills as well as my strategic ones, all made sense to me at the time—and still do now. But oh, have I learned some things about us as marketers & advertisers along the way.

In a country of sheep, it pays to be one most of the time. Whether it's a long-lasting hangover & dry-mouth brought on by *tall poppy syndrome*, or it's a facet of the stiff upper lip mentality, I learned very quickly that being successful is okay—as long as you're not too proud of your success. I can remember becoming friends with an Olympic gold medalist who literally had to say, "Yeah, nah. I'm pretty proud," when asked about winning his medals (MULTIPLE GODDAMN GOLD MEDALS, PEOPLE).

I asked him, "Why didn't you say how proud you were of yourself after dedicating YOUR ENTIRE DAMN LIFE TO YOUR SPORT only to win & be universally known as THE BEST IN THE WHOLE WORLD at what you do?" He looked at me, erm, sheepishly & shrugged. "Cass," he said "they'll eat me for lunch if I even pretend to be proud of myself. Tall poppy." That broke my heart. And it helped me to set an intention in my life that still rings true to this very day.

Tall poppy? Yeah, okay. Sure thing. If that's the label you need to embrace to be proud of your accomplishments, so bloody be it.

In a 1998 song by the band Cake called "Sheep Go to Heaven, Goats Go to Hell," the band crooned the lyrics:

As soon as you're born you start dying
So you might as well have a good time, oh no
Sheep go to Heaven
Goats go to Hell
Sheep go to Heaven
Goats go to Hell

Through these seemingly inane, yet surprisingly chipper lyrics, we're reminded that society tells all of us that it's not okay to step outside of our predetermined societally constructed boxes. We're born into communities that give us preordained guardrails & tell us when & how to stay in our lanes. If we're good little sheep, we abide by the rules. If we're not good little sheep, we're goats. And goats surely don't get the good stuff in life (though they are the originators of some delicious flavours of feta cheese the world over). Nah, goats are baaaaaahd, to the bone.

The intention I set after that heartbreaking chat to my Olympic buddy? Tall poppies be damned. If sheep go to heaven, I'm not keen on heading there. With a foundation of kindness & commonsensical attitudes towards building people up without having to take them out at the knees as well, I headed into my life & my profession. I knew full well that there would be many people who wouldn't be as comfortable with being themselves, with openly celebrating the successes of others, & with being honest about how bloody wanky we can all be sitting around boardroom tables, if we don't call ourselves & others out around the bullshit that sometimes comes out of our mouths.

I'd be lying if I said that we, as marketers the world over, are great at embracing others for who they are & celebrating successes with open hearts. Nah, there's always a wee bit of side-eye & an underlying current of tiny-foot-stomps where egos feel bruised for not having won some kind of industry award that only matters to industry people (who usually fudge results, anyhow). We've got a whole lot of work to do in realizing that we're the best placed people in any part of any business to truly celebrate each other.

We're the storytellers, the data scientists, the insights mavens, & the gurus of glittery iteration—imagine what could happen to business & corporate cultures worldwide if we stopped acting like sheep & started poo-pooing the well-trodden paths blazed by ad-men in times of simplified media channels.

What would happen if we all decided to take a step or two off the tried & true? Even if it's muddy, murky, & leads us nowhere new, we'd have a story to tell on the other side. When thinking about the state of our profession right now, I'm reminded of a job interview I went for almost a decade ago. The position was a mid-level marketing manager position working for a pretty big retail brand here in New Zealand.

After making it through a few first-rounds, this final meeting was with the "big cheese." I was excited to meet a woman in leadership & really hoped we'd hit if off when it came to ideas, potential, & looking towards the future. Instead, I got a cold-fish handshake, a constant checking of her watch, & was handed a GIANT SPREADSHEET with colours & timelines on it.

This spreadsheet was more complex than the one used to launch NASA's first rocket into space. The boss lady's only question to me was "Can you read this?" My response: "Yep, but tell me more about the way you strategically build out stories & creative iterations for your different customer sets."

From the look on her face, I'd gone too far. *Oh dear baby Jeebus, we've got a non-sheep here! We've got a thinker!*

***CODE RED! CODE RED! CODE RED! ***

Soon after this little parlay, we shook hands again; this time her grip was firmer. So, too, was my resolve not to work for that business at that time.

If marketing at this company was all about colour coding spreadsheets & being a lap-dog for spoiled agency men, my answer was simple—intentional, even. Nope. Nah. Nuh uh. Thank you for your kind offer, but that was not the place for me. I mean, yay for the Excel whiz-kids, but also boo for the reliance on defining skills by how pretty you can colour in boxes that will never be adhered to.

I have always needed more when it comes to who I work with. If leadership isn't inspiring, how in the world will our work be? This interview was a turning point for me: I learned that I had a choice in where I worked. Having a job title that other people saw as important did not make me an important person. I am so happy I learned this lesson young. I am also happy that my time spent between two childhoods reminded me that, sometimes, you need to look beyond the sheen to understand the nuance of a place.

When we talk sheep v. goats—not the real animals, obvs—I think about either sitting on the shore watching the waves roll in or paddling out amongst the whitewater & learning to ride them. Far too many of us think the safest place to be is on the shore. But I'd argue that it's not.

There's some kind of comfort in knowing terra firma is beneath you; however, I'd rather live my life knowing that the shore will always be there—but there's never the same wave twice. Every drop of water, every pull of the moon, every set that rolls underneath you teaches you a new lesson. Whether you need to duck below a wave that's breaking too soon, bail on one that's going to drive you into the ground, or reach a perfect rhythm with the tide, you're learning. You're adapting. You're getting stronger.

As marketers, we cannot safely sit on the shore & observe the waves. We need to grab our boards, paddle out, & get amongst the magic. If we remain sheep, we remain shallow. And if there's anything surfing & marketing teaches us, it's to get in over our heads if we're going to enjoy the ride.

EFFICIENCY OR EFFECTIVENESS?

For years & years, we've all watched as the digital revolution not only changed how we work, but also how we define success as workers. Though we may not be bees out to produce the largest amount of honey, we're definitely chasing objectives that are just as sweet. As with anything shiny & new, our industry has been inundated with charlatans who are out to swindle us, & good actors who have the most amazing of intentions to help us—both in equal measure. Between the two lies a common thread: the need to constantly optimize & make our processes, strategies, & actual outputs more efficient.

In reality, we're all stuck in the hamster wheel of *doing*. Most of us are happy here, too. Admit it. It's comfortable popping & dropping tried-&-true strategies that give us tenuous glimpses of growing a bottom line. Spinning our wheels: it's what we're actually doing. Dissecting information, as long as the information doesn't require a deeper look or a new approach.

Looking at numbers that feel fuzzy & warm, we forget to dive into the end of the pool where our feet can't touch the bottom. Hell, we can't even see the bottom when we stop playing the safe game.

Sure, when it comes to safety, we're really good at mastering the hamster wheel. What would happen if we all just all hopped off the wheel & took a look at things as they are? Why would anyone run, run, run, & be happy with getting nowhere? This is modern marketing to a T when it comes to efficiency taking top priority over effectiveness.

What do I mean by efficiency overtaking effectiveness? First, we're caught up in WIPs, RASCIs, BAU, & every other anagram under the sun—other than WTAF! We spend bazillions of dollars (yes, that much—maybe more) on tools that promise to optimize our performance.

We bring in consultants to help our teams become more agile & to streamline efficiencies without ever asking, "WTAF are we doing all of this for?" I hate to break it to ya this way, but being efficient does not make you effective. Not in the least. And it is effectiveness that drives business growth & longevity. Even the most agile of businesses can fall victim to their own brilliance when the brilliance is laser-focused on the wrong target.

Shift to Productivity over Process
Peter F. Drucker was an Austrian-born American management consultant, educator, & author, whose writings contributed to the philosophical and practical foundations of the modern business corporation (I pulled that directly from Wikipedia—sue me). Peter was also a badass. I've read a lot of his work, & although he wrote some of it over half a decade ago, the heart of his pondering still holds fast when it comes to business success & how to build for it.

One of the best quotes Drucker ever wrote is also a guiding principle for me. When Drucker wrote, "There is nothing so useless as doing efficiently what should not be done at all," a big 'ol penny dropped for me. When I feel myself getting wooed back on to one hamster wheel or carnival ride, I am able to stay the course.

To pause, to pivot, & to prepare for change often. In actuality, what does it mean to put effectiveness (productivity) over efficiency (process)? First, we as professionals must be able to make a distinction between efficiency and effectiveness. Simplified right down, efficiency is about getting the maximum amount done, but effectiveness is about getting the best results.

I completely understand how we've put so much weight on efficiency over time. Our modern world has increasingly become a bigger-is-better & more-is-better kind of place. BOGO. Sale culture. Consumerism gone awry. When our wants became affordable at scale & our needs became simply *met*, the idea of getting more shit done/made/sold quicker was the pinnacle of business. And of marketing.

The good news is that we're all starting to see the detrimental effects of consumerism gone mental. Plastics are being banned; products are being made ethically & sustainably more often. Yet, a lot of businesses are stuck in a place of wanting to change, but not knowing how. So they invest in efficiency without understanding their most effective business models.

The most important way of approaching business now is to listen to Drucker when it comes to dialing up effectiveness. The lure of brand-spanking-new sparkly platforms, processes, & acronyms is easy to understand. These promise us short-cuts when it comes to productivity & scaling a business or brand. TRUTH BOMB ALERT: there are no goddamn short cuts. None.

I hate to sound like the naughty Aunty at Xmas who drinks too much eggnog & tells the toddlers that Santa isn't real... but the truth is that we all must earn our stripes. Every single one of them. In life & in business, climbing Everest happens one step at a time, one foot in front of the other, regardless of year/ gear/or who's pushing you from the rear (metaphorically speaking, obvs). Sure, you can hire a helicopter to take you close to the top... but you'll only ever reach the peak & understand the climb by putting in the hard work. To do this, we need to consistently question why we're doing what we're doing & dig into discernible results.

Miley Cyrus was right all along: it's all about the climb. Also, a party in the USA is a always a good bloody idea! Rock it, gurrrrr-rrl.

SLACKers & Distractions
There will always be someone willing to write a book (or ten) about doing business better by doing business differently. No matter the fancy packaging or attempt at inserting a sense of newness to an old process, new tools that become oversubscribed without first diving deep into why they may help a brand or business are usually more snake oil than second coming. A few quick things to do, right here & right now, that can help you shift to a more effectiveness-based model of business is to start with the meetings.

Meetings, when undertaken without thought or care, are soul killing, time-wasting effectiveness & efficiency stealers. Seriously. How stressful is it to look at your calendar the night before your next business day & see ten hours of meetings lined up back-to-back? Without purpose, intentional outcomes, or the ability to be more efficient (here's where efficiency rocks), you're blowing it.

As Drucker noted in some of his writings, *"The key to running an effective meeting is to decide in advance what kind of meeting it will be. Different kinds of meetings require different forms of preparation and different results."* Seems like a simple premise, right? So why do we spend so much time in hour-long meetings that aren't extremely purposeful? I think meetings make us feel busy & feeling busy makes us feel important. The truth, though, is that busy doth not a productive marketer make.

The next time you receive or send a meeting invite, why not try something my good friend Aaron Ward taught me a decade ago: always have three bullet points. The first is WHY you're having the meeting. The second is WHAT you're looking to achieve in the meeting. The third is WHO needs to attend & what is expected of each person. Most meetings can actually be done over email in a few short sentences. When it comes to filling your diary, less is oftentimes more, Team.

Let's change gears away from meetings & talk a little bit about connectedness. For a long time, e-mail has ruled our professional lives. I can remember life before email. Seriously—if you're a fringe millennial like me, you might just remember signing up for a Hotmail account when Hotmail was brand-spanking new. Back then, e-mail was a novelty.

I remember sending my first email to my high school best friend Kendra & was so happy to get a reply, three days later! In the intervening three days, we'd seen each other 1,000 times, talked on the phone just as much, & spent time going to basketball camps. Ah, the good old days before email became someone else's to-do list for you. It was a passive platform. Somewhere informal to share little snippets of fun or information. It was not a harbinger of crowded weekends & even more crowded thought patterns.

To beat back the deluge of time-wasting that email has wrought on modern business practices, new communication platforms like SLACK, SKYPE, Facebook Workplace, & thousands more have popped up—all promising more efficiency & effectiveness of workforces. Promises be damned; whatever your tickle of choice, these little bots & bringers of supposed efficiency actually work to lessen our focus, & thus, our productivity. Don't believe me, though: I have science on my side.

Studies have shown that when we work with apps like SLACK open at work, our ability to concentrate on any one task is reduced to 40 seconds. FORTY GODDAMN SECONDS of concentration. If we've got more than one app or messaging platform open, this drops to 35 seconds. No wonder it takes us for-freakin-ever to write a creative brief or to pull together a post campaign report that is pithy enough to mean something to the business.

We are so inundated with tools meant to help us be more efficient & productive that we've over-pivoted & are now twisting ourselves in pretzels, wondering how to turn towards effectiveness again. My tip? Turn the bastards off. All of them. Most digital tools now have airplane mode or something like it where notifications are placed on silent.

If you travel often & you're like me, airplane mode is akin to a slice of quiet heavenliness. There's beauty in travelling without distractions or feeling like I need to jump online to make sure someone hasn't pinged an inbox that loves nothing more than being empty.

Over time, I've learned to flip the notifications off. No messages, no emails, nada. The truth of the matter is that if someone really wants to get in touch with me quickly, or if there's an emergency, they find a way to get in touch. Whether it's walking to my desk, actually going old school & ringing me, or something else—there are ways. By ensuring I work in a (mostly) distraction-free digital environment, I am a gazillion times more effective than I would be otherwise. My mind makes space to think creatively & objectively. My work is better.

Ask, Review, & Revere Change

There's something beautifully jarring in questioning your own biases & asking other people "*Why?*" often. I love to learn, which is why I ask a lot of questions. I also loathe the status quo when the status quo doesn't allow for growth. I'm all for opportunities & taking them when they present themselves. Most of the time, a business does well when it brings in the geeks, the outliers, & the people not afraid to ask the most pressing (& usually most obvious) questions. With diversity of thought, diversity of process, & strong data, a business thrives. Without these things, it stays afloat at best.

While I love the magic inherent in storytelling & the cadence of languages, math is still very important when you're a marketer. By crunching the numbers often (from what I've read, six monthly seems to be best practice), you're better placed to know which products are driving the most return for resource required to sell them.

Dial these heavy-hitters up. Oftentimes, we spend a lot of time for very little result. While efficient processes might cut down on time & resources, results speak. Find your sweet spot, focus on it—don't fear ye olde pivot. It takes both boldness & bravery to walk away from that which no longer works. The Wild West was only wild for so long. To conquer new ideas, territories, or to win new customers, you MUST try new things... often.

THE GLORIFICATION OF BUSY

If you're like me, your life is a bit like a hamster wheel —built specifically for our human legs & cardiovascular machines, but not so much primed for healthy minds or souls. We live out our best years as worker bees, bound by a monotonous & perpetual cycle that has been colloquially dubbed the 9-to-5. I say colloquially because we all know that, as marketers, we'd love an actual 9-to-5. I've often heard typical working hours called out as "Gentlemen's hours." Ahem, gentle-people. This is 2019.

As children we're told that to be successful, we'll need to be a part of cycle, a cog in the proverbial wheel if you will, to be a true success. So, we work hard. No one can take our toil from us. But why do we do it? What is it about a flashy, creative title that intrigues us? Is it the award potential, the pats on the back, the metalware sitting on the mantel at home that reminds us of how clever we are when wielding a pen or buying ad placements that get lucky?

So many of my fellow marketers aim for the top. They forget how important they are as individuals who were put on earth to do other things than to get lost in the mire of retail—simply so that, one day, they might be graced with a trifecta of holy letters

—CMO.

We give our all to it & we lose out a lot of time, sleep, adventures, milestones of our children, & dreams to it. If we're 100% honest with ourselves, whether we're working in retail, banking, entertainment, travel, media... you name it... we're all the same. Hesitant marketers or proudly "out" marketers, our modern professional lives begin each morning in traffic on the way to the office & end each evening in the same way (but in the opposite direction, obvs). We see little of our families & even less of our friends. We connect online passively & see children growing up through the lens of our smartphones.

At work, we're busy, dammit. So, so busy. We run, run, run on that human hamster wheel until our legs & minds are almost at breaking point. When we get to such a state of exhaustion, integral aspects of our strategic minds start to sit down on the sideline for a breather.

When we're so intent on putting one foot in front of the other for fear of crashing & burning, what we lose is perspective. Surely the most important part of running the race is taking in the course around you? But tunnel vision kicks in. We forget ourselves, & often we forget the people we're trying so hard to impress: our customers. All of this because we, as an industry, glorify the hell out of being *busy.*

Burnout. Anxiety. Other mental & physical disorders brought on by stress. They're here & they're gunning for all of us. As groan-worthy as this is going to sound, I need to come clean. I myself have suffered quite the millennial burnout (this is a real, documented *thing*). Let me tell you, friends, rock bottom isn't a beautiful place to fantasize about. You don't fall down & then magically get back up, wipe yourself off, & then have a great story to tell once you hit another pinnacle on the other side of the climb. Nope. Rock bottom is shitty & shit-filled, & more often than not, it's a place where we break into a million tiny pieces. Some of which never get put back into place.

In reading up on how we can stop chasing our own tails & demystify the beauty that we're told dwells in the act of being busy, I've found a lot of scientific studies (not to mention a lot of non-scientific ones) that point towards the beauty of boredom. Or, rather, in just *being.* The art of being still for the sake of being still has a lot of names, & in our society, which sees standing still as something akin to laziness, most of them have negative connotations.

But not "niksen." To the Dutch, niksen is the idea of purposefully doing nothing. And this idea is my stillness-Bae. At the heart of it, adding moments of *doing nothing* makes a lot of sense. Taking the time to do things that seem wasteful of time —like staring out of a window (not weirdly at other people, that's creeper territory) or sitting motionless without a screen in front of your face—are important acts of self-care. When we daydream or allow our minds to wander without boundaries or pure intent, we allow ourselves to embrace the way in which our own individual minds wander.

Fun!

Modern workplaces have breaks built into the day, yet we rarely take breaks. As someone who's been in the corporate game for a looooooong time now, I didn't start taking breaks until recently. And even then, when things get (AHEM) busy, I push my quiet time aside in favour of meetings, spinning wheels, & random deadlines that I exhaust myself over to deliver.

If we all know that we need to slow down, why is busy-work something we still brag about? When did *keeping up with the Jonses* take on the tonality of professional time-wasting? Slowing down is the new luxury. Stopping for a moment to catch your breath & clear your mind: pure bliss.

As much as we're a smart crew as a collective, we keep fanning the flames of exhaustion & setting into our foundations bad habits that will follow those that come after us. We don't slow down. We refuse to slow down. We keep running headlong into burnout because if there's one thing we love to brag about in today's uber-connected & fast paced world, it's this: man, we're BUSY! But WE MUST STOP THIS UTTER BULLSHIT WAY OF WORKING & DYING.

As for me, my give-a-damn was busted a while ago when it comes to letting everyone know how busy I am. I mean, halle-fuckin-lujah, right? As a fantasist optimist (yes, someone called me this once in a way that was meant to wound... it didn't), I reckon we can stop the humble brag that masquerades as martyrdom. In the past few years, I've taken formidable & intentional steps away from the glorification of busy.

Most days, I wake up before the rest of my household & wander for a good 15 minutes. Wander? You mean, like, walk around & wake up slowly without any aim whatsoever? Yep. That. It's a bit like meditation, without the Namaste & the ohms. And for me, it works. After my body & brain are both awake, I spend a few minutes identifying moments in the day that could be simple time-fillers/wasters. You know them well, I know you do.

They're things like those three hour-long meetings about meetings to identify time to have more meetings? They can be sneaky, too. They waft into your calendar in a state of back-to-back 30-minute WIPs without you even knowing. And if you can't decline them beforehand, you're forever known as "that person who declines meetings at the last minute." So yeah, I flat-out decline time-wasters when I see them come in & even when I don't.

Most people know my boundaries well enough now & send through three bullet points about what they need from me & I get back to them pretty quickly. This makes life easier for all of us who survive by filling in requests for people above us on some marketing org chart. Let's talk about this part of the culture of busy, too. Folks at the top (whom I truly believe to be mostly well-intentioned) walk into a room on Tuesday asking for yellow roses, then change their mind on a Wednesday & want them red.

The flow-on effect of lackadaisical decision making is a shit-ton of busy work that is ineffective. For all of us who lead & make decisions, I beg of you: think about the impact of your words, moods, & directives. DO NOT CREATE MORE PILES OF BUSY WORK FOR PEOPLE TO DO. Kthxbye.

Right, ranty pants are off now & I'm back in something a bit more comfy & less confrontational. The way I look at my work flow & effectiveness for a company, project, or role comes down to what is expected of me & what I deliver. I truly believe that e-mail is merely someone else's to-do list for me, & I refuse to answer the call of paper shuffling in the digital age. When prioritizing my work, I get to prioritize my day. When I think about e-mails, I believe that if someone really wants me to dive into solving a problem, they'll ask me specifically & add a timeframe to the delivery of whatever it is that they're after. It is not my job to be a desk junkie who sits awaiting a little *ping* of supposed importance when another communication rolls into my inbox. I dunno about you, but inbox zero is my happy place. Perhaps my Montessori-style childhood grew me into an adult who doesn't sit well with banality, or perhaps I am personally hardwired to needing structure in my work life; either way, I've started to unpack *busy* for myself & for my colleagues. But how?

Well, first, let's look at language. We've already identified that (as a collective) marketers love a good colloquialism or bit of slang to keep us glued together. When it comes to glorifying the time-fillers, we need to recognize when we're using language to put lipstick on the proverbial pig. Dress it up all you want, but each time someone says *"I'd love to help, but I am so stacked/busy/ full up..."*, a magical marketing fairy dies in the Forest of Creativity.

When you hear yourself saying anything like the above, check yourself. Stop in your tracks. Put down the spreadsheet and simply be present. It's amazing how much you can get done when you focus on one thing. Drop the busy. When I think about all the time we waste as desk jockeys, running from meeting room to meeting room in an attempt to get in our 10,000 steps, I think of Tim Ferriss & his *4 Hour Work Week*. Now, I should say straight up, not many of us can simplify productivity down from 60 hours a week to 4 hours, but why not aim for something that allows us to do less, better?

Beyond the language we use to dig deeper foundations into a soft earth beneath us, we need to stop praying at the altar of Busyness. Being busy is not a badge to be worn proudly, it's the opposite of such. Restfulness, taking time to think through strategy & projects, & building in space to be creative is necessary now more than ever in professional spaces.

If doing less but outputting more was actually a "thing," wouldn't everyone be opting for it? You'd assume so. But, nope. We've been trained to think that quiet time, idle time is time wasted. But without it, how are we, as creative & strategic beings hellbent on creating awesome work, going to find the space to create? We need time to allow our minds to think critically. To wander creatively.

The first iteration of an idea is usually never the best—but most days, it's all we've got. We don't question constructively for fear of becoming busier still. We fear what we desire: being busy. Which leads me back to kindness. And to being our best selves at work & at home. In a fast-paced industry, the best thing you can ever know is who you are. Without a title. Without a corner office. Without a uniform on. Who are you, after hours?

Don't worry if you can't pinpoint your passions beyond your

profession (actually, worry, but do something about it). I can't stress the importance of spending time, of getting all Namaste & diving deep into thy self.

The SELF. Getting to know yourself means you'll be more engaged, confident, & driven across all aspects of your life. You'll also have a much more attuned bullshit monitoring system when it comes to playing the game of glorifying busy. When asked to half-ass a project or to twiddle your creative thumbs for the sake of it, you'll know when to say "no thanks."

You'll reclaim your time.

And you'll be a much better & more productive marketer for it. Promise!

Take time to explore the world beyond your daily routine.

ALWAYS LEAVE THE OFFICE ON TIME

I recently read a story on LinkedIn titled "Always leave the office on time," & it resonated with me deeply. Not just a sweet-fix click-bait headline, the article itself was a deep dive into the reasons we all should have strong boundaries around our personal time & our professional time. I have always believed in putting our spiritual self ahead of the self that chases titles & praise.

First before all things, though, is family. The promise to put family & self before work is one I think we all make—whether we shout it from the rooftops, meld our working hours around it, or whisper it like a silent prayer—we inherently know what's important in life. And usually it's not busywork or BAU.

That said, marketing is a beast unto itself. We place so much pressure on our own shoulders & the shoulders of those around us that it's difficult to not be reduced to an anxiety-ridden worrywart when life happens. You know the feeling, right? Your child wakes up vomiting in the middle of the night & you realize you will have to miss THE BIG MEETING. The one that you've been prepping for *forever.* The one than might make or break your career. You wrestle with guilt—you know you need to stay home cuddling a small, feverish human—but your brain is in overdrive trying to figure out how to juggle both.

So, you never really log off, shut down, or leave work. Ah, our modern lives. Ever connected, ever interconnected. Technology is our biggest helper, but also our biggest hindrance when it comes to finding our elusive necessity: balance.

If you've made it this far in this book, I'm sure you've got a good feel for my sense of humor—and also for the passion I feel in recognizing our humanity at every step of our collective journey. Whether you're marketer or marketee (or just a normal human who wanted to pull back the covers on what marketing is really like), there's so much beauty wrapped up in constant, subtle nods to that which fills our souls & makes us believe in ourselves just a little bit more.

In the marketing game, we spend a lot of time trying to convince other people that we're cleverer, more strategic, more efficient, & more forward-thinking than others. Don't roll your eyes at me, ha! I can see you doing that. We DO spend most of our time preening & peacocking around—polishing awards & paying tribute to glory days of yore when we wrote *that line.* You know the one. The one that launched not a thousand ships, but shipped a thousand products.

Luckily, we're a pretty fantastic family of quirky pros. Loveable rogues, I'd call us as a group. That said, we're as imperfect as we are clever. Always overachieving, always over-indexing on how much time we spend in the office. I can't even begin to count the times in which my ego felt a little pat-pat of approval when I'd be first to the office to turn on the lights in the morning & the last to leave in the evening. Nary would a day pass when someone would slyly insert into mundane conversation that *they had been toiling longer & harder* than anyone else that day. Yep, we all know who gets to the office first. And we all feel a twinge of jealousy & guilt about it. Well, not all of us.

It's taken a few decades of soul searching & enduring come-to-Jesus moments that brought me no nearer to Jesus at all to have a fairly anticlimactic truth drop in my lap: time in the office does not equate to better work, better marketers, better brands, or better results. What we're doing when we spend our time racing against the clock (& then watching it all day) is simply getting good at writing rules for efficiency, for a game that we need to win with effectiveness instead.

By marching in time with the clock, by ensuring that the maximum time we spend as desk jockeys becomes the new daily minimum, we lose our lives to someone else's hustle. And that someone else is not the person tasked with great results. What I've learned over time is that egos have no place in marketing. They get in the way of brilliance.

They devour us whole. When it comes to the time we spend on our profession, we dive deep & stretch widely. In some cases (I shit you not), we hand out actual awards for the people who valiantly give up their weekends to come in & fill out spreadsheets or create pivot charts for post-campaign reports that might never see anything other than the bottom of a recycle bin.

Yet, we carry on.

For me, the carry-on has gone on too long. I used to be embarrassed to call myself a marketer. In titles or introductions, I asked people to call me an "accidental marketer" because I loathed the implications associated with the word & the profession in equal parts. I didn't want anyone to think that I was playing the game of whiling away the hours just for the sake of it while I could be out seeing the world & gathering new inspiration & human truths to apply to our frequently over-hyped strategies.

In the last two years or so, I've realized that I am most effective (as in "delivering great work & getting work done") when I am balanced. For me, balance is about time. Time to wander, time to ponder, time to focus, time to ramp up the intensity. Time is our most precious commodity as marketers, yet we only pay homage to its passing instead of stepping back & being more intentional around how we as individuals & collectives can work in with it.

As an individual, I work best when I am given a problem to solve or a task, then am allowed to work when & how I work best. At times, this means that I am up at 3am, furiously making & breaking hypotheses while tying neat little bows of creative execution to seemingly everyday advertising outputs. I am not asked or pressured into giving up my time with family when I can work towards a goal.

I am also able to be much more self-aware in group situations when it comes to teetering on the edge of burnout. A quick run outdoors or a walk down for a coffee is all it takes to find space between the work & the clearer side of life. Without balance, we will all fail. We all need time & space to experiment, learn, & explore. Long days notching up bonus points that mean naught IRL keep us chasing our tails.

As a leader, I never have & never will ask my team members & colleagues to work late. If deadlines are looming & we all need to push harder, then we do. But never will deadlines be more important than family.

But if we're all a part of the proverbial machine, how do we as a collective ask for—ahem, demand—better working conditions for everyone? How do we make it the norm to leave early if we arrive to the office early? How do we stop the back-chat & grumblings of those who aren't quite woke when it comes to understanding that time in the office does not a productive person make?

Well, the first part is to realize a couple things:

- We are not born to be machines.
- We are born to live & to create.

Once we have these two ideas are tucked nicely away in our back pockets & embedded in our marketing psyches, the next step becomes less tenuous & instead, more intentional.

Being intentional can take on so many different meanings. For me, it means being focused & aware. When I bring people on to do a job, I tend to be super commonsensical about a role & a person's ability to undertake & deliver upon the objective of said role. If I need two people to do a job, I hire two.

Or if I can't have two people (we all know the strife inherent in "frozen headcounts"), I assess the business needs & work toward the most important need. By doing this, I can hire one person to focus on important & effective jobs to be done. Right now, our industry has a lot of catching up to do when it comes to putting humans ahead of random deadlines.

My way of working is that if you get in early, leave early. Ya know? I've spent far too many years working 14-hour days for big companies who just expect extra effort without putting any extra effort into me. Where's the value exchange in this kind of lifestyle? No wonder Millennials & Gen Z are calling for better from businesses. And no wonder old-school businesses are scared shitless of a future workforce who demand more in terms of purpose, outputs, circular economy, & heartcounts.

Not long ago, I had the honor of attending the funeral of a colleague of mine. Mark was young, too young, when he passed, & his life ended without warning. As in all celebrations of life, we heard stories of Mark's childhood, his teenage years, & his adult years. His service was very well attended by colleagues, family, & friends. People recounted stories of a life well lived, & laughed & cried while talking about the heart of the man who was no longer with us.

I've always been a crier. Every family has one, & along with my Aunt Cynthia, I cry in good times & bad (& have also been known to cry when certain county music songs play on the radio!). There's a saying about saltwater being the most healing substance on earth: I believe it. Anyhow, as tears rolled down my face in paying tribute to a fantastic man, I was reminded just how short life is. I was also reminded about how much time we spend at work.

Never have I been to a funeral where someone says, "Here lies so-and-so, he/she sure put in a lot of extra time on those P&P ads over weekends. Sure, their family missed the time with them, but oh, you should've seen our click-through rates!" I hope I never hear drivel like this, either. Arriving early & staying late is not a badge of honor, a sign of martyrdom, or a fast-pass through ye olde gates heading into the Kingdom of Forever. One of the things that helps me remain steadfast in leaving the office on time is thinking about my own funeral. Not in a morbid or weird way, but in the sense that I'd like to be remembered for more than my job.

When we remember people, we remember them for their big ideas, their big adventures, their big love, their bigger quirks, their individuality, their kindness, & for how they touched us all in individual ways. There's always a memory of that time they danced on the table at the Cowboy Bar to Tina Turner's *Rolling on the River* & gave themselves whiplash (okay, just me on that one, then?). There are tears of joy in missing the nuanced person beloveds were able to glimpse. But NEVER should life be about someone else's hustle. Ever.

When I think about leaving the office on time, I also think about the people who counter arguments with "But I love my work!" To which I say "Cool, that's rad! Yee haw & go you!" But even the most creative brains need silence & change to grow. Becoming one with your job title & filling space with busywork that could be filled with adventures leads to unfulfilled lives. It also leads to creatives who really aren't all that creative.

Look around you at the most revered & successful people you know —I bet you a buck that they know how to "turn off" & to turn their hand & imaginations to pursuits that stretch beyond working longer hours.

Holidays & time off are like gym sessions for the soul. Take a break, clear your mind, & your work will be even better when you're back at it. If you're just "sooooooo busy," I get it. However, there comes a point where you deserve to stick up for yourself & say yeah/nah. You deserve to be at your very best, & I can guarantee you the best marketers & professionals on the planet are people who know when to knuckle down & stretch to meet a goal, while also knowing when to turn off & rest.

If there's one thing you should do to be a great marketer, it is this: always leave the office on time.

SLOW DOWN
TO SPEED UP

Hustle, hustle, hustle. There's nowhere left anymore that's sacred enough to thwart the onslaught of the hustle. We're inundated by the need to run faster, to keep up with the proverbial Joneses. And in the game we're playing, there's always someone willing to shame someone else for not hustling harder today than they did yesterday. Earlier, we talked about the glorification of busy, & it warrants repeating that hustling hard does not an effective marketer make. Hustling smart, or rather slowing down to speed up, does.

How can that be? Well, sit back & relax for this chapter, my friend; I've got a few stories to tell you about the importance of tending your garden & slowing down to do so.

Goodbye, Commute. Hello, "Me Time."
I recently had three weeks at home between jobs. Well, really, only one week between them—but I spent the last two weeks at my old job tidying up & tying up projects from home. But that's all beside the point.
Regardless of workload, what I got was three weeks of not having to fight traffic, rush out of the house, or stress about attending meeting after meeting without time to eat, drink, or

pee. The aforementioned stressors are what I call the *Trifecta of Natural Losses* in the modern corporate world. I can usually do without food or water for eight hours... but I can't stress the importance of building in toilet stops into your day if your calendar is chock-a-block from hour to hour.

Right, back to my three weeks "off." I know it wouldn't surprise you to know that a professional life without traffic, timeframes, interruption (open-plan offices can be both the best thing & the worst all at once), or the need to wear anything other than activewear is good for both mind & body. I must mention that my use of the word *activewear* is—like spandex itself—stretchy. Some days, I was happy as a clam to roll out of bed at 5am (I am an early riser, always have been) & don my fake UGGs, polka dot fluffy robe, & geek glasses from dawn to dusk. Oh, the freedom in scorning pants & makeup.

Whoa nelly! Life turned a sharp corner & went from full speed & full-on to productive, passionately paced, & precious. All it took to learn the beauty of slowing down was a few weeks of working to my own timeframe, at my own pace. I learned to focus—I'm talking *laser freaking focus*—on jobs to do. I also learned that having the freedom to exercise or simply do the laundry during brain-breaks dialled up my ability to think more strategically, creatively, & deeply.

My goal in having time between gigs was simple: I longed for (needed) "me time." I needed space to do nothing or everything —whatever my heart & mind felt, I would follow. All those copy-paste days of waking up, getting out the door, driving to work, sitting through meetings that could've been emails, driving home, sleeping... wash, rinse, repeat... they left me exhausted. My soul needed filling.

I longed for nothing. Clear space. A wandering mind. Learning the art of *doing nothing well* was the pinnacle of re-setting for me, or so I thought. Because as it turned out, my idea of *nothing* became doing a lot of *somethings*. And looking back on it now, I've learned some good lessons when it comes to the art of slowing down to the speed of life.

Meditation in Motion

What have I learned about slowing down, then? Well, firstly, I've learned that walking—or rather, wandering—without reason or end goal is the most cathartic thing for me when it comes to clearing my mind & moving my body. I so love wandering. For 21 days straight, I walked. Yep, every damn day for three weeks, my body moved where it would. Uphill, down dale, near the ocean, in town. In doing so, I felt a huge shift in myself, both mentally & physically. I put my phone away & looked at flowers. I relished in the sunlight on my arms & legs. I sat near the ocean. I even became "that person" who sang along to my iTunes shuffle while walking down a busy street, happily looking like a nutbar, without giving one single damn about the side-eye stares from strangers.

I went to cafes & eavesdropped on little old ladies (holy-freakin'-moly, can old ladies gossip!). I got to know the local dairy owners & revelled in their stories. I discovered the beauty of podcasts (oh god, Oprah, I love you!), And I rode the ferry to town & back to discover new back alleys & lanes I'd never seen before. In all, some days I walked over 30kms. Never did I have a day under 15kms. And the wander + ponder gift I was given by having & taking the time to see the world new again cleansed my soul happily & helped my mind to create more.

There's peace in allowing your brain to wander freely. When you realize that there's life beyond office politics, chasing numbers, & exhausting yourself to the point of tipping over, you put more onus on chasing memories. We're all only ever here for a short time. We might as well make it a good time. Right?

Wandering for the sake of it is akin to re-learning to play. At some point, as adults, we deprioritize playing. Some of us (I'm guilty of this at times) forget to play at all—or we create an internal narrative that playfulness at work will be seen as weakness. Pish tosh to that crap. My goal moving forward? Play more. Laugh more. Connect more. What a blessing to have time to play without boundaries. With the only reason for it being to have fun & be joyous. I believe 110% that there needs to be more time built into corporate life for people to work play, physical movement, & the space for thinking into a day.

Slowing Down Means Speeding Up—Creatively

Between & during walks, & whilst getting myself ready for speaking events & workshops (that I also shoehorned into my "me time"), I listened to hours upon hours of podcasts with topics ranging from the *science of happiness* to *building engaged teams* to *LGBTQ+* rights conversations & beyond.

By listening to other people, other points of view, & diving deeper into topics & conversations that interest me, I was able to think more broadly. To ponder. To pontificate.

Most mornings, my friend Wendy would come for walks with me & we'd end up with no ears between us (because, ya know, we talked them off of each other). What I found from having more unstructured learning, more fluid conversations, & more time to dive deeply into different topics is that my creative mind flourished. Like a garden, you must tend to your creativity & mental health for flowers to bloom. It's almost as if the walls of big business act as force-fields against creativity; they crush the flowers that are fighting to blossom before they're ready to.

Really, though, it's not the walls that cause many of us to think inside of the proverbial box: it's the constraints on time. Creativity & cleverness both take time. For amazing work to happen, we need air to breathe, time to settle in, & space to evolve. And a knowledge that speed does not equal best results, by any means. Just as we nurture those we love, we must learn to nurture ourselves & our own ways of working. We must honour the individuality inherent in each other, because the ways in which I work best won't always be the same as the ways in which you feel most free to do your best.

By binging the *TED Radio Hour* with Guy Raz, *Queery* with the amazing host Cameron Esposito, & a handful of other amazing podcasts, I filled my mind day in & day out. And in doing so, I felt myself becoming more & more interested in the world around me. Slowing down, for me, was a reawakening of sorts.

No Phone, Who Dis?
One thing that happened the last week of my "break" was that I became homeless as far as mobile phone plans go. YES, THIS SHIT STILL HAPPENS IN NEW ZEALAND! For a full 8 days, I had no data loaded onto my phone. None. Nada. Nothing. When I left the safety of free Wi-Fi at home, I was on my own. No texting. No Instagramming my daily #scoot. No distractions.

Days one & two of no data were the most difficult for me. I didn't realize how addicted to my tech I'd become or how reliant I'd been on the interaction of others to quantify my feelings of self-worth. It's amazing how often we all pick up our phone & look at it for no reason. And I mean NO REASON AT ALL. We've hard-wired (ahem, for us older folks, re-wired) ourselves to have our little BFF in our pockets or on our person at all times. And I'm being real here: there were moments where I almost struggled to put my phone in my backpack & just leave it there. I had to force myself to leave the phone in my pack & even started some self-talk to remind myself that I'd be okay without human interaction in a digital format for a couple of hours.

By day three, everyone who needed to get in contact with me (or might need to) knew I had no connectivity unless I was at home or in a public place with Wi-Fi. The freedom of knowing I wouldn't hear the dull pings of emails, text messages, DMs, or social media notifications while I walked was awe-inspiring. I was no longer on anyone else's timeframe. I made the rules in my day around when I would check emails, when I'd answer messages, & when I felt like turning back on to the tech.

So, what's the point of all of these words? Why praise the art of wandering aimlessly for an entire chapter?

Easy: we all need to do more wandering & pondering. We'll be better professionals & even better people the more often we log off.

We live in a world where the *exaltation of busy* is the way in which we comport ourselves day in & day out. I reckon we all need to ask for (perhaps even demand) time to slow down to the speed of the wind in the flowers, the bees in the trees, & the cadence of lyrical gossip that flows from the mouths of old ladies in cafes at lunchtime.

When we allow ourselves to do nothing, something becomes of it. If time is our most precious resource, we need to be kinder in doling it out to ourselves on a daily basis. We also need to be able to realize when we're moving too fast, too often. Climbing off the hamster wheel of life & running beside it—then out the door—is the best way to stay hungry, creative, & able. Demand space to create. Reclaim your time!

I hope you're able to enjoy slowing down soon; you deserve it.

INFLUENCE
SCHMINFLUENCE

We're living in a modern world where we're drowning in a glut of useless, valueless, banal content. Online, offline, in line—there's no escaping advertising telling us that we need to buy more, throw away less, & be our most individual selves whilst walking the strong lines of societal acceptance. We bathe in the waters of thinly veiled diversity, only to realise it's murky mud that we've been splashing in all along.

In amongst the drudgery (a lot of which we, as a profession, need to answer for) & content that we're blind to before it's even pushed out into the ether, there are some bright lights of valuable information, giggle-inducing dad jokes, & cultural references that help us feel better about ourselves. These little nuggets of gold give us hope. Rather, they give us a quick saccharine-sweet fix. Quick on the tongue, quicker in the body. Devoid of nutrition meant to strengthen the body.

With the open nature of & onslaught of creative shoulder-charging, a new era of marketing & advertising has been ushered in over the past decade. This new era features the democratisation of information & the ability for anyone with a smart phone & internet connection to put ideas out into the world, without boundaries. And sometimes, without bounds. We over-share. We become addicted to red notifications when they pop up. A COMMUNICATION! I MUST BE IMPORTANT! Our brains are wired to seek out more pleasure, & social media was built knowing this.

Which leads me to the parts brands & individuals play when it comes to the economy of influence & the power of reaching bazillions of people quickly (for some), or not reaching anyone at all. The beginning of social media ushered in a time of seem-ingly greater connection between people, brands, & traditional media; however, the inherent openness of platforms meant that bad actors, trolls, & egotistical grabby-pants jerks has made the online space that started out promisingly one that now needs governmental intervention to police it.

We're all standing together on the precipice singing "Kumbaya." Soon, though, it'll be sink or swim. The game is constantly changing. By the minute, hour, day, week... forever & ever, ad infinitum.

On the whole, we're all accidental players in a game that's gain-ing a whole lot of traction. A game of influence. This game isn't like any we've ever partaken in before, as a collective. Sure, we've played others where we didn't know the rules or the end objectives. But this one is different still. As brands & as the keepers of brand stories, we're changing who we let tell our brands' stories & how.

This is both extremely promising & frightening. We play the game because everyone else is, & because stopping seems like an option we wouldn't be able to live with. But why? Have we thrown out the proverbial baby with the tepid bathwater in an attempt to corral cultural relevance on channels we don't own? I'd argue that many of us are doing just that.

Influence Schminfluence. I don't know about you, but I'm tired of picking my eyes up off of the floor once they've rolled out of

my head after someone with a moderate social media following & an even less moderate engagement rate introduces themselves to me as an *Influencer.*

Yes, an *Influencer* with a capital "I." Sweetheart, unless you've
got transferrable skills & a plan for the future that reaches beyond the top five social platforms as they exist right now, you're
not fooling me. You might be fooling traditional marketers &
those blinded by flashy new toys. But yea, nah. Not me.

As part of my day job, I work a lot with communications
& PR teams, counseling them on strategies for engaging with
folks who have fairly good reach & even better engagement
across communities that we're hoping to level with. Too often,
though, brands still look at influencers as new, cool, sparkly, & a
little bit unknown. But I know the truth. Oh yes, I know.

To be influential at all, someone must be able to actually
influence others. Hashtagging your short-term love for something you don't really love is disingenuous. Consumers aren't
the dummies that marketers seem to think they are. There's no
pulling the wool anymore, Team. Actual real-life-humans are
ahead of the game because they're the ones making up the rules.
They're the ones changing the rules. And they're the ones who
are agile enough to pivot away from anything that's not completely authentic.

When it comes to socialising with, briefing, or otherwise inter-
acting with people who call themselves *Influencers,* there are
only so many fruity cocktails, selfie-angle-lessons, unboxing
stories, & boring chats about authenticity I can take before I
want to throw myself out of a window. Seriously!

Case in point: I was at a launch party for a new, hip retail brand in
Auckland a few weeks ago. The invite list for said launch party
was a who's who of B-list celebs & C-list social media influencers. I'm not meaning to be a Debbie Downer here, but every up-
&-comer that I was introduced to floored me. Not in a good way,

either. I've had to smile & nod through a lot of professional bull-shit in my time, but this night took the cake. Took it, smashed it, & walked out with it on the bottom of its brand-new Gucci shoes.

You see, not one person took the time to ask questions about "non-influencers." They talked, and they talked, & they talked. But it was all about them. It was about THEIR followers. THEIR communities. THEIR content. THEIR goals. THEIR genuine ability to connect. THEIR take on a world they have little to no experience of walking. Snooze fest. When I asked questions about skillsets, value added to the lives of others, & the ability to walk away from social media, I got blank stares in return. Bless them —a big shot of reality is just on the horizon for folks who think that talking to an Instagram story makes you special or important.

The actual definition of influence is *the capacity to have an effect on the character, development, or behaviour of someone or something, or the effect itself.* As someone who's worked in sponsorship branding, I can tell you that you must have some sort of genuine cultural relevance beyond a channel itself before a brand & your community will truly value the craft you put out into the world. You cannot fake, purchase, or hijack cultural relevance. Well, not in the long term.

There are hacks & short-cuts, of course. A simple one is to get yourself cast onto a reality show. From there, short sighted marketers can (&often will) mistake your growth in followership for a power to influence. Oh, the come-to-Jesus moments that our industry will face in the near future! Right here & right now, I am making a bold call: we must all work harder to understand cultural relevance & the part we play in it. Once we understand these things, we'll be much better suited to understanding how, when, why, & whom we should be working with as long-term brand ambassadors. Short-term shouldn't be in your terms, Team.

Don't just believe me, though—believe science! Study after study tells us that we are swayed by people we trust before anything else. In fact, a peer recommendation is more valuable than any ad. Also, there are no ad-blockers for IRL conversations with people you trust.

Yet we marketers still spend a huge amount of our time & resource on ad placements. We pray at the altar of best practice for platform, we sup at the table of Google, Facebook, & Instagram, hoping to hack algorithms. And we over-pivot on building clever iterations of one-off product & price ads instead of investing in customer experience, sharing narratives that matter, & connecting with truly influential community leaders.

We're missing a powerful strategic imperative here, friends. We're being wooed by the big boys. All the while, we're undervaluing people, reducing our customers to data points. By doing so, we're setting ourselves up for mediocrity & a shit-ton (yes, that's an actual numerical term) of wasted money spent on influencer partnerships that people are blind to even before a single pithy quote is posted to Instagram.

Why is this? When you boil everything down to one source of truth, you get the conundrum of time.

We're drowning in content. Actually, if I am completely honest, we're drowning in a tidal wave of shitty, banal content. The numbers are staggering. If you went right back to 1960, there were 82 minutes of content available for every minute used by people. For every minute of human life, there were 82 minutes of media to consume. THAT'S WAY TOO MUCH. But wait, it gets crazier. Fast forward to 2015, when the figure sat at a staggering 2,000-plus minutes of available content to every minute of humanity on earth. *HOLY CONTENT SATURATION, BATMAN!*

There's good news & bad news about these numbers when it comes to influencers. The good news for humanity (because I am an unshakeable optimist by nature) is that we have such a vast excess of media available compared to our needs, we as consumers can afford to be very choosy about what content we engage with.

The bad news for marketers & brands is that people who aren't our brands or our uber-fans inherently value less the contribution of any commercial sponsor in bringing us content we don't need. And believe you me, if I haven't already hammered this point home clearly enough, I'll say it again: brands create a lot of horrifically useless, valueless, & boring advertising. Because of that, even the good stuff gets ignored a lot of the time.

So where to now, for influencers & the economy of influence? Like ethically sourced products, the process for working with experts, ambassadors, or short-term influencers should be circular. We should understand how our communications—even those undertaken on our behalf by others—affect the lives of others. Once we understand this, we should dedicate our professional lives to purposes that build positive value into the lives of many. We also need to hone in on building trust in the long term.

Building trust is an always-on, intentional brand strategy. Every business I know that puts trust at the centre of their marketing absolutely kills it when they wade into the waters of working with influencers & their communities. Hands up if you remember the world in which the word "YouTuber" didn't exist (HAND SHOOTS UP!).

The first time I heard the word, all I could think was that it sounded less like a professional content creator & more like a custom-made potato. Because I was in the throes of working long hours & raising a small human at the birth of the YouTuber movement, I've always been a bit less dazzled than others by the implied power in becoming a professional unboxing champion.

Over the years, though, I watched as influencers grew into a "maturity" of sorts whereby they yielded the power of free reach & eyeballs. When this happened, brands were chomping at the bit to claim a piece of the advertising puzzle without having to pay the big bucks that media platforms were charging at the time. Enter YouTube's golden years.

I'd be remiss if I didn't make mention of the OG influencers. Creators like Hannah Hart, who were (& still are) equal parts deliriously cute & inspiring, learned as they went. They zigged when the world zagged. They hustled hard & realized that a free ride wouldn't be a long one. Ah, if only all influencers were like Hannah!

With time came a watershed few years where any kid with a webcam tried to outsmart YouTube's algorithms with the end goal of being so crazily popular that they'd find riches & fame without really having to try hard. Some YouTubers came into themselves. Most, though, ignored the fact that they'd need transferrable skills to be worthy of big bucks in the long run. They believed that they were owed payment for online stardom.

As I watched this unfold over the course of years, I became pretty frustrated. I also felt old. Who did these upstart whippersnappers think they were? They hadn't seen the world, they hadn't experienced anything... gah! *shakes fist at the sky* Nope, sitting in your bedroom, pontificating into a low-quality webcam whilst lacking actual human or life experience does not a guru make. But even today, many label themselves as such.

Most influencers forget about the need to perform. No matter your profession, we all must perform. Performance pays: performance of self; performance of channel; performance of marketing objectives. Many people played to this—and then fell over flat when channels started changing & algorithms started to throttle reach & payment because of it.

Around about the time that algorithms started pissing off their main creators, I started spending time at VidCon. Truth bomb time: I was cynical about a GIANT conference built on web celebrity. I mean, wanky. Right? Nope! I got the surprise of my professional life when I first attended & saw the scale of community brought together around the idea of creating. Of making. Of exploring individuality.

I learned very quickly that, even in very densely crowded spaces filled with thousands of big stars & someday-hopefuls, you can see the true professionals a million miles away. Sharp-minded humans who are just as sharp-witted. My heart pitter-pattered a little bit with joy. I started to drink the proverbial Kool Aid for a few days before heading to quiet Manhattan Beach to walk for hours on end & think through what I'd just seen.

In very macro terms, I came to the conclusion that it's the elder group of influencers who are some of the most potent people on earth. These are people who truly wield influence & who are very intentional about how they use it. Community. Connection. Growth. Change. They work to build people up & to add value. While I've seen quite a few of the first generation struggle with understanding their relevance in a world where reach is throttled, the true influencers out there are committed to more than a passing need to hack algorithms for personal gain.

I reckon that the moment influencers started calling themselves such, they began to fade from actual relevance. The only thing that get better as it fades is a good pair of jeans.

My main tips are simple for building strategies that matter around influencers:

Understand your business goals & lean into them creatively.
Don't work to singular flash-in-the-pan campaign goals. Focus

heavily on your business goals & work with experts, ambassadors, & influencers to lift these stories over time.

Think long term.
Sure, you can interact with & sign campaign-specific contracts with influencers to create little bursts of reach. But is reach all you're after? Surely you're more woke than that. To add oomph & value to the reach you're chasing, make sure you're playing the infinite game. Building trust is two-way & takes time. Don't rush strong relationships.

Don't try to hijack cultural relevance.
Work hard at applying creative thought to interpreting cultural movements. From there, work harder at finding magical points of intersection where your brands & product stories sync nicely with the narrative of culture.

Woo people.
To do this, you need to communicate purposefully with your audience by treating them like humans, not soulless datapoints on a hashed spreadsheet somewhere, locked in the belly of a CRM system. When building your media strategy in relation to influencers & brand, ensure your content is emotional in approach, consistent in application, & broad in reach.

Always, always tell measured, intentional stories.
We understand & make sense of the world through story & metaphor. Humans, even the most seemingly rational ones, aren't rational or logical at all. When we identify with real people & real stories, our brains get super happy! Our mirror neurons fire off, which in turn, heightens emotional connection (this is why we love reality TV enough for it to turn normal folks into *Influencers* overnight).

Invest in Influence.

Do your homework & spend time getting to know the people you're looking to work with. Every time you hire someone else to advocate for your brand, you must know what these people are passionate about. Getting to know the influencer you're keen to work alongside means hearing their own goals, desires, & fears. Pay people what they're worth, too. Great content costs. The old saying, "Pay peanuts, get monkeys," is one that I have on repeat when it comes to understanding that nothing comes free. Value exchanges must have both parts: value & an exchange. Invest in the best, get the best.

I LIKE YOU, YOU'RE DIFFERENT

How many times have you arrived at work & rocked into the office, only to realize that you & four of your colleagues are dressed in exactly the same outfit… again? I can't even begin to quantify the times I've walked into a meeting, agency pitch, or workshop to see a sea of sameness. The funny thing that's always happened to me is that the colleagues I end up dressing like are the dudes—not the beautifully dressed professional woman.

Nope, it's the dudes & me. (I guess there's something about black jeans, a flannel shirt, & leather boots, eh?) A thousand times, I've heard the quips, "I see there's a new marketing uniform!" & "Bitch stole my look, lolz…" & a thousand times, I've cringed. I am a goddamn individual. I am the only me! *Le sigh* Yet, I'm not. None of us are really all that individual. Human survival has always depended on safety, community, & clans.

This is why you can walk through almost any large business the world over & point out the different teams simply by what they wear: there's the IT team (polos, slacks, black New Balance shoes), the HR team (power suits, approachable tops, & painted on smiles/grimaces), the marketing team (wingtips, funky black bespoke everything), the creative team (no shoes, hats, torn jeans, harried facial expressions). We find our people, we stick with them. We embrace the comfortable because it's, well, comfortable. But not me.

Comfort isn't what I've ever wanted out of life. Instead, I've actively chased things like excitement, wonder, adventure, connection, & love. Life is just so much grander & filled with so much more grandeur when we force ourselves to step outside of the beige & into a tie-dyed reality.

Over the course of my working life, I've always gravitated towards the outliers, the weirdos, the nutty professors, & the gurus. I've searched out uncomfortable situations, knowing that discomfort is the only way I'd learn how to stretch who I am & what I know over time. All I know now is that I don't know very much. Growing up, I had friends of all different backgrounds, races, creeds, & beliefs. Having playmates who weren't like me heightened my awareness of the beauty of nuance. I loved how funky, individual, & interesting my friends were. Talk about a creative bunch of misfits.

We played our own games, we broke every single rule, & we built strong foundations in helping each other make our way through the world. Beyond the good stuff, having a diverse friendship group also taught me very early about the many forms of inequality in the world. I saw how unfair a lot of shit was. Especially adult shit. Political shit. Racist shit. Misogynistic shit. Homophobic shit. I hated it then. I hate it now. I'll always hate unfairness. It's shit.

To combat a sense of dread around humanity & our hard-wiring to put ourselves & others into broad groups of *US vs THEM*, I actively sought out stories from people who lived lives completely different to my own. In searching out stories told by people with different words, different narratives, different heroic journeys, I found myself.

In fact, every time someone tells me something about their worldview that shocks or surprises me, I find myself anew. I find myself asking questions I'd never thought to ask. And I find myself working even harder to ensure that my workplace is built upon the fundamental pillar of diversity. When I talk about diversity, I am talking about diversity in its broadest sense. Diversity of thought, of background, of race, of sexual orientation, of culture. Intersectionality isn't a trend. It's a belief & a way of living. A way of working better, to better serve a more diverse & connected world.

When I think about what I know & what I don't know—the truth of the matter is that all of us have a skewed view about the breadth of knowing that is possible in the world. The more we are around different people, the more stories we hear that are different to our own, the wider our self-awareness is when it comes to our current state of personal *not knowing*.

Realizing this early on meant that I became comfortable with being the least knowledgeable person in most rooms I entered. I voraciously took in new information, tried new things, & asked millions of hard questions of people who I knew would have different viewpoints than I already held. Setting my ego aside meant that I got to shine a big spotlight on the passion I've always had for leadership, for building teams, & for coming up with creative solutions to storytelling across new & traditional media platforms alike.

Boiled down to the simplest terms, opposites attract. They also build strong, successful teams when placed in the right environment. Case in point: *Team Awesome*.

Our friendships. Our intentional ways of being a true team, a unit. A FUCKING GODDAMN UNIT. Five strong women doing the heavy lifting of driving business & brand positivity, while also staving off the attacks of teams coming at us from all sides.

We needed to know everything about each other & nothing at all. We tried our hardest. We trusted each other with our lives & our livelihoods. We became, very quickly, a family. And more than anything, we thrived with each other.

We couldn't have been more different.

Meet Gee:
Gee was always going to be one of my favourite people on the planet. She has kind eyes & swagger that would make Kanye bow at her feet. She's a wanna-be mafia boss. Quiet until you get to know her. Once you have her trust, she becomes one of the funniest, sassiest humans in a 100-mile radius. When I first started my job, Gee was on a secondment from another team. After having her for a week, I knew we needed her. When she went back to her original team, I wasn't having any of it. I fought like hell to get her back. It could only be Gee in that seat. It could only be Gee to fill the role that she was always meant to fill.

Her unique skillsets. Her opinion, her viewpoint, her way of just getting the job done, bringing innovative solutions to the table, & real-world way of speaking to us while treating customers as worthy humans. There wasn't a single day I wasn't thankful for Gee. Without her, we would've fallen flat on our faces so many times; because of her, we had solutions. Gee kept pretty much to herself, she got her work done, & she led by example. She put up with my qualitative view of a growth mindset.

And she allowed me to sing Snoop Dogg without making me feel like a giant dork (I am, if anything, a giant dork.) Over time, Gee became my go-to when I needed a temperature check of the team. She was honest but didn't sugarcoat anything. If I fucked up, she'd gently let me know how she'd attempt fixing things—while still making me super aware that I'd better fix things.

My daily work goal was to make Gee roll her eyes. She has a very high threshold for idiocy & bullshit. So, to get Gee giggling or rolling her eyes at Dad jokes is a compliment in itself. Gee never backed down from a challenge; she never met a problem she couldn't find multiple ways to break down to solve. As a leader, Gee was connective tissue. Even when she was going through her own struggles outside of work, she came in & treated our entire team like family. She always took me at face value—treating me with the respect of a manager, but with the love of a friend & leader.

When I told the team that I'd left my husband & that I was pretty stressed at home while going through a divorce, it was Gee who placed a card on my desk late at night for me to find when I came into work the next day before anyone arrived. I still have her card. I still re-read her words all these years later. And yes, I'm a wimp... I still cry thinking about the kindness of Gee.

On paper, you couldn't get more different than Gee & myself. But that's the beauty of living life: we don't live on paper, we don't thrive based on labels, boxes, stats, & key skills. We live & breathe in creativity, empathy, kindness, & shared experiences. The things that made my story different to Gee's are the things we both found joy in. To this day, Gee is still the coolest "G" I know. I love the kid, & I am so thankful for our differences.

Meet Clarey:
Oh, where do I start with Clarey? Maybe I should start at the end—or rather, where we are right now. Clarey is in New York City, living out her creative dreams, in love with a handsome Irishman & with the woman she has become over the past few years of bumps & turbulence. Clarey's Instagram newsfeed is a snapshot into the golden-drenched summertime of a life she's building for herself. I am so proud of her, I could just burst, literally. Though we're 10,000 miles apart right now, we're sisters for life. Dreamers building empires with hopes of them merging gracefully.

But if you need to know anything about what Clarey & I share, it is a lack of gracefulness. I'll explain: neither of us have figured out gravity yet. In fact, the thing that brought us together not just as colleagues but as family-by-choice almost always centered on one of us falling down or oiling newly tattooed eyebrows (that was me, I am a ridiculous human sometimes).

Clarey & I started at the same company a week apart. Because of that, we bonded. Our collective introductions consisted of a small list of paper with names on them & a pat on the head with the directive, "Go on then, go well..." We found our way through the corporate maze before us, thanks to the rest of the team. We also sat next to each other. From day one, this meant endless snort-laughs, creative sessions fueled by passionate storytelling, & a customer focus that was 100% built upon common-sense melding with data & empathy. Though Clarey is a decade younger than me, we worked very well together. Whether it was words, images, video, or the perfect death-trance backing track for a happy story (yeah, we love it when the bass drops), we found a way to tell stories without ego, without pride. Because we both worked in a space that was meant to drive others to feel inspired, we felt inspired.

Over the course of a few years, we learned each other's language when it came to courage & creativity. We learned from Gee, Mimi, Kaksha, & Joansie. We worked with the wider business. But really, we grew up together in completely different ways. Through heartache, broken marriages, & all of the wild cards that come with lives that start to unravel, we became stronger. More than anything, we trusted each other with stories. Then, when it was appropriate, we shared similar stories to help build up other people. Being in a storytelling role was akin to being in a healing role. I don't know if I'd have survived as well as I did without Clarey. We still talk/FaceTime/message each other daily.

Again, finding the beauty in that which made us different built a genuine bond that no time or corporate restructure could ever unravel. If Clarey has taught me one thing in life, it is this: we must all value stories more than any other thing on earth. It is through stories that we survive & thrive. Without stories, there's no business. There's no marketing. There's nothing. Own your story. And when others entrust you with theirs, do right by them in the telling of it.

Meet Mimi:
Take one part German efficiency, one part cake-maker extraordinaire, & one part curious cat—mix them together with a swirl of kindness & hilarity, & you've got Mimi. The first time I met Mimi, I knew she would become family. I mean, *I knew it.* It was like kismet for friendship. There was just something about the honest way that Mimi looked at the world & looked you right in the eyes that made me think this human being would be someone I could trust & truly get to know. Luckily, that little voice that whispers in our ears & tugs at our guts was correct.

From the get-go, Mimi was hungry for knowledge. She sought out opportunities to learn & grow. And she was fearless in asking questions. Fearless. In fact, Mimi never once came to any meeting (be it one-on-one with me, or in a full room) without her notebook & at least one page full of brilliantly bullet-pointed questions. So ferocious was her quest for knowledge that I couldn't help but feel lifted when working alongside her.

I should note here that Kiwis, as much as I adore them, aren't the most forthright people on the planet. If dancing around direct questions & answers were a sport, these beautiful folks would be gold-medalists on the world stage. Move over, rumba; sashay away, fandango... Kiwis are the best there is when it comes to dancing around directness in conversations—mostly the hard conversations, too. Which to Mimi (being German) & myself (being American) was something that was difficult to fathom.

We both saw the world through a lens of *"If you don't ask, you don't know."* How were we to know that asking was offensive to so many people & so bruising to small egos? Anyhow, Mimi & I learned quickly how to spot the two-stepping around subject matters & how to jump right into the dance to help as best we could.

As much as we were similar, we were, & still are, starkly different. Mimi finds beauty & joy in details. She's a whiz at spreadsheets & she is meticulous. I sometimes can add extra fluff to conversations & struggle with pivot charts—but together, wow, we became two pieces to the large puzzle that made up the beauty of our team.

Even after I left the business we worked at together, Mimi would ride in to work with my wife & me in the mornings. When she needed guidance with work, life, or anything else, she'd arrive to the car with a smile & a, "All right, we have 15 minutes together... I have a list for you..." & she'd bring out her bullet points for us to go through before the day began in earnest at any kind of office. Mimi is a soul-filler. She's a smile-bringer. She's what the world needs more of.

Mimi even baked my wife's & my wedding cake when we married on Waiheke Island on the first day of summer. Ever my beautiful friend & meticulous German, Mimi practiced the cake a few weeks before our big day & brought the whole family around the most delicious cake I'd ever eaten—well, up until that point. The following cakes that she made & decorated for our wedding were somehow even more delicious. Maybe the story of Mimi getting the cake to the Island & then to the venue helped with how delicious it was.

She protected the cakes within an inch of her life, & her fiancée couldn't help but giggle once she'd gotten them safely to the venue before the ceremony. It was at that point she could stop &

breathe. We're so happy Mimi is a part of our New Zealand expat family!

Meet Kaksha:

Kaksha was my *old soul*. Of all of the women on the team, it was Kaksha who looking into & right through me from day dot. While our rapport was immediate, she was someone from whom I knew I'd need to earn love & respect. In our first team meeting, it was Kaksha who was bluntly honest with me about the state of the team prior to my arrival—let's just say the times were trying, at best, before I came on board—Kaksha let me know it without a dancing around the subject. For her honesty, I loved her immediately.

Because of the position I was in, it would take longer for her to love me in return as someone other than simply her manager. That said, it wasn't years or anything before we developed an amazing relationship at work. Kaksha was then, & still is now, one of the funniest & kindest people I've ever met. Coming from a traditionally Indian culture & having married into another traditional Indian family, she cares for others in a way that I've only seen in my life a handful of times.

Kaksha helped before & after work in her in-laws' business & quite often cooked for large family gatherings. She never came into work without a smile on her face, though, even when I could tell she was absolutely exhausted by her duties outside of work. When it came to learning & curiosity, Kaksha thrived.

She was a North Star of sorts for the team, & even for me when I needed help finding my way back to a happy or optimistic frame of mind. We couldn't have been more different on paper, but over the course of our working relationship, we became family. Forever Family. What a blessing honesty, nuance, & individuality are in life!

Meet Joansie:

Ah, Joansie! Our wild card! Joansie came on board to run our Chinese social media channels. Because none of us in the team spoke Chinese, we didn't have a full understanding of the proverbial tools she was working with. This meant we literally had blind trust in her from the moment she sat her bum down in her chair. Joansie was a good fit for the team, too. Coming into the fold a bit later than the rest of us, & having to learn all of our quirks while working in another language & with a huge subtext that linked her to an entire other culture, you couldn't blame her if she didn't enjoy working with the rest of us.

Let's face it: sometimes, when you are a new member of a tightly knit & mostly sarcastic crew, it's difficult to feel part of the inside jokes. Actually, it's difficult to feel part of the team at all. But, that wasn't Joansie's way. Nope, she worked her butt off to be a part of the team, on & offline. If anyone taught me patience, understanding, & finding humour where sometimes there wasn't anything overtly funny to snort-laugh to, it was this amazing human. Joansie grew in leaps & bounds; she opened up to us & trusted us. She became family very quickly.

Like the rest of Team Awesome, Joansie found her rhythm & stride alongside the rest of us. To this day, I am still grateful for the completely different way in which she saw the world. It made coming up with strategies, spotting potential holes in plans, & creative iteration more inspirational!

Ah, magical times.
Ah, magical people.
Ah, magical happenstance.

I know not all teams can work like this—this team, this time, this context was one part beautiful happenstance & one part utter magic. With Team Awesome, we were gifted to each other. Randomly, perfectly, imperfectly, & all at once. Working in safe, driven, compassionate teams is what we all long for.

Work will always keep, deadlines will come & go, but the beauty is in the nuance. If you can do one thing consistently for the rest of your working life, let it be that you celebrate the differences in all of us.

Fall on the floor laughing.
Stay curious.
Show up for each other.
And when shit times happen (because if anything is assured in the marketing game, it's that shit times will happen), keep showing up.

The rest is icing on the cake—or oil on the eyebrows. Whatever tickles your fancy.

C WORDS

I f there's anything I love in work & life, it's a good deep-dive into C-words. LOL. WTF? Yeah, welcome to my mind. Always a bit left field; but that's cool, left field is my favorite position on the old baseball diamond anyhow. Seeing that I was born a literal C-word, and seeing that "C-Word" was once an actual nickname my ex-husband's ex-girlfriend lovingly called me, it just makes sense to feel close to them. To me, C-words just feel a bit warm, cuddly, & slightly badass. Think about the beauty of the C. Cookie. Clever. Caboose. Capsize. Cheeky. Chuffed. Climax. Cervix—a ha! Caught ya sleeping, didn't I?

As a young girl, Cookie Monster taught us that "C is for Cookie, that's good enough for me!" And if any song has ever helped me through life, it has to be this gorgeous wee love letter to cookies. That said, I'm not here to talk about Sesame Street, ditties, or naughty words that march along in 4-lettered-giggles.
Nope, I'm going to dive a bit deeper when it comes to Cs. These Cs are the ones that might make or break a brand, a person, or a profession. Since I'm addicted to the rosy-colored outlook of life, we'll be focusing on the things that can make your business stronger, your soul fuller, & your journey through your profession more successful.

Buckle up, Team. Here come my fave C-words!

CREATIVITY
Defined *as the use of imagination or original ideas to create something,* creativity is my C-word Bae. It's easy to fall in love with a concept that melds together originality & functionality. It's also fun to live & work in a profession where the art of crafting a strong strategy & marrying it to clever creative iteration is soul-filling.

Within the bounds of creativity are abundant opportunities to not only find clever ways to deliver marketing & ad campaigns that are both effective & memorable, but there's also a spark of magic in moments when all of the pieces of a proverbial puzzle come together.

Call it what you will, I know instinctively when I've had an "A ha!" moment. By rights, as someone who can live in big blue sky while still acting as a tether to the reality of business needs, creativity is what keeps me going. I've been reading a lot of articles recently on the future of work, on the impact of AI on marketing, & on crucial factors for driving business & individual success in a saturated digital marketing world.

Of all key attributes & skills required to drive success, I bet you can guess which is the stand-out winner. Yep, head & shoulders above anything technical, creativity is what we need to start teaching our young ones to embrace if they're going to be successful as they grow.

I should also be completely clear here as I write this. I'm not talking about teaching our sweet young people to be like the presumptuous, wanky, assholish once-were-super geeks who style themselves as savants & name themselves "Creatives" with a capital C whilst looking down on anyone who doesn't have the ability to wear tight leather pants or to sit around all day drawing on walls & calling a scribbled storyboard "art."

Nope.

There's a fresh hell reserved for the creatives who actually believe that their minds are better than those of others. The truth is that every single one of us can be taught to be more creative. We can wire our brains for strategic thought, & we can also wire our brains to think beyond the norm—to love playing in the realm of ridiculous.

To do this is pretty simple: we create a cheat sheet (we marketers love a good cheat sheet, don't we?). Dialling up creativity in any situation can be done in five simple steps. The first step is to understand the problem you're attempting to solve & understanding *associations* between questions, problems, or ideas from other fields.

When you can look beyond your product or campaign to another & see connections with the idea you're attempting to harness, you're on the right path! From associations, the next move is towards *questioning*. Early on in my career, I often fell victim to building ideas upon wobbly foundations—or, rather common wisdom.

It's the job of a creative mind to question common wisdom; to poke at it, to shake it in the box, to break it a bit. When it comes down to it, newness only happens when we step away from the old ways of thinking & doing. Therefore, questioning is critical. From here, we must take the time to *observe* the behaviour of customers, competitors, stakeholders, & suppliers. When we watch others, we often are able to visualize just how things might be done better, more efficiently, & more effectively. If we skip the observing phase of creativity, we miss out on crucial information when building ideas that meld originality & functionality.

Networking, like observing, is a process by which to introduce & challenge new ideas for people who see the world differently to you & your team. At this point in the creative process, it is key to ensure that your networking & working groups are diverse. Diversity isn't just a catch-phrase for modern times, my friends, it's a necessary ingredient to being successful.

There are only so many of the same faces & places we need to re-hash before everything becomes banal & yawn-worthy. After networking & sharing your concepts wider than the team you work most closely with, you've now reached the *experimenting* phase of your creative journey! This is where you get to pull together all of your strategy, information, iterations & ideas, & try them out.

The best & worst part of the creative process is sharing what you've created with others. It's exhilarating & horrifying, sharing something you've created with people who might not see your vision through eyes that understand the method to your proverbial madness. But it needs to happen. Brilliance that isn't shared is brilliance wasted, yes?

Embrace that fear, my friends. Share your ideas, & as you do, take people on the same journey that you went through in conception. The sell-in is much easier when people understand how you made it from David Bowie to a pair of skateboarding sneakers.

I couldn't write about creativity without including a strong nod towards those moments we all have when we just can't get into the groove of creating. We're all different when it comes to how we create, too. Some of the most brilliant creative minds I've ever worked with can create on the spot, in a room full of people.

They feed off of the energy in a room. I can't do this. In fact, situations in which I am put on the spot to deliver brilliance scare the shit out of me. I need a more hybrid experience. I need time to myself, to work through the first few steps of the creative process, & then I need others during the networking & experimenting stages to optimise ideas & executions.

Knowing that we all thrive in different environments is key to being a successful leader & a successful marketer. When I need time away from the hustle & bustle of the office, I walk. I leave the noise & head outdoors.

I find there's no better way to understand & embrace a wandering mind than to wander. While wandering, I am able to focus on a singular problem & to hone in on a single source of truth that leads to many ways of approaching a solution. Whatever it is that helps you find your creativity, know your levers & pull them when you need to. We're all creative & we're all creatives. All of us.

So own your creativity.

Own all of it & be proud of whatever brilliant ridiculousness your mind conjures up. Author Liz Gilbert has summed up creativity & the pursuit of living a creative life in a way that I am in love with: she calls it *Big Magic.*

And I'm all for this kind of magic.

COMMUNITY
Talking of magic, another favourite C-word of mine is the glue that holds humanity together. Beautiful, imperfect, necessary, & strong; without community, we'd all be wandering through the world alone. I remember when social media & online chat started to seep into daily life. I was in college in Santa Barbara & my roommate, Carrie, downloaded AOL Instant Messenger. The interface was so easy, the ability to connect so quickly was novel, & the feeling of community was immediate.

As silly as it may seem now, we actually used to chat to each other online while in the same room! Not long after discovering the ease of community building when adding people into chat streams & conversations, the first murmurings around Facebook started. We already had MySpace. Why did we need/want/ require something other than MySpace?!? LOL. Oh, how interesting it is, looking back on the days before the big blue logo!

It was my younger brother, who was in school mid-way across the country in Missouri, who invited me to become a member of The Facebook. My first reaction to the new platform was reluctance. My second reaction (very soon after the first) was happiness. I could see people I know who were super far away from me & check in on people around the edges of my community, too.

IRL & online really started to meld into one. And for a while, the social part of social media reigned supreme. When it came to community & community building, it was all of us together. Before we, as a media & advertising profession, over-pivoted on shouty advertising in a traditionally community space, we stayed fairly kind to each other, too.

But things, as they do, changed. From my perspective, change is good. It's constant. It's the only thing promised to any of us. But somewhere along the line, over the past decade, with a glut of social media channels finding their way into our brains, we seem to have forgotten the heart of what matters most for people as a whole: the connective power of community. In the past year, I've lost a handful of men to depression & anxiety. All of these men were young.

They had young families. They were talented. But with the pressure to keep up online with the likes, comments, shares, & witty retorts, they lost a true community. For them, even with all the connections available online, IRL was a lonely place. My heart breaks for those they left behind. My soul longs to do better to ensure community is the centermost aspect of any connective outlet we humans are a part of.

So, how do we dial up community in an era where ad units, whiz bang interactive ad placements, & more ads hit us on the daily than ever before in human history? Well, first, we need to invest in our people. Who are our community managers? How do they see the world? Are they taken good care of, both on & offline?

Once we as marketers & business people learn to treat the online world as a place just as beautifully suited for building positive interactions as offline, we'll literally be saving lives alongside driving business return. Not a bad combo, right?

Also, when it comes to community, taking the time to banter & have fun as a brand is of the utmost importance. The gorgeous reality of the democratization of communication in the form of social or online media is that we're all able to connect better & more frequently on our own terms. We're able to see, hear, & invest in truly diverse ways of seeing the world. Basically, community managers who do an awesome job at their jobs are some of the most woke & empathetic people I have ever met. And if we can shift the conversation to business performance for a hot second, community is the root of all sales. It always has been & always will be.

This is why there are creative agencies out there who are still attempting to peddle "viral videos" in response documents. They're not just going to make you a video. Nope, they're after virality. Why? Simply because social currency & viral sharing are things you cannot buy. They're at the upper echelon of the community scale online. They're Wonka's golden ticket. The only way to cash in your ticket is to invest in community. There are no more happy accidents & social media shortcuts. Humans are mostly immune to bullshit. So why not turn away from the BS & dive into authentic community building? No matter the channel, platform, or space—if you have an engaged community, they'll follow wherever you are. And that is magic!

CHANGE

Ah, ch-ch-changes. Turn & face the strange indeed. When it comes to the most impactful C-word of them all, change has to be it. Change is our only constant. It is both a North Star of hope & a black hole painted in shades of despair. Everything & nothing all at once, change is what every movie, song, story, & creative endeavor is about, at the core. And cliché or not, change is both the cause & effect of everything any of us ever do in life.

Which means that getting comfortable with it—or rumbling with it, as Brené Brown might say—is the only way to live a truly fulfilled life. It's in the rumbling that we build muscle memory & mass. It's where we gain grit & strength & maturity.

If we spend our time at home, at work, & at play afraid of change, we'll spend our time in a constant state of fear. And bleurgh. Yuck. No one wants to live like that. Embracing newness & seeing opportunity in change takes practice, though. It also takes communication. When we talk about comfort & joy, a lot of the words that we weave into societal narratives are those of stability & relative sameness. We love the idea of jobs that don't go away, homes that are forever homes, & families that never veer away from what popular culture tells us families should be. I call bullshit on all of this.

When you think about growing up, what are the stories you tell yourself & others? Are they banal stories of days that turn into months that turn into years that become a life of doldrums & sameness, or are you a bit more like me & see your defining moments as the ones you could never have seen coming? When I was a kid, there's no way I would have guessed that I'd become a professional storyteller living on the other side of the planet in a country smaller in size & population than my home state. I'd never have guessed that I'd marry young. I definitely never would have imagined that I'd be a young mother, or by rights, a young(ish) divorcee.

Going through the pain of a broken marriage meant that all I knew was change. And I had to get comfortable with it on ground that I wouldn't ever describe as common. Far from home in a country that didn't raise me, I came of age because of change. I became a better mother because of change. I became my truest self through a complete unravelling. I learned that love wasn't stagnant, but a rollicking ride. A rodeo ride of sorts. One minute I'd be racing around barrels, then there'd be eight seconds of sheer bull-riding terror. All up, though, life's been one helluva rodeo. That's all thanks to change.

There's something superbly beautiful in embracing the grit that comes along with the pearl of change. When it comes to our work, the most important thing we can do as professionals is to embrace the changing nature of communication platforms & to try our damndest to love little moments of newness that shift & change our goalposts daily. The world of a successful marketer is a world in which change is seen as a curveball that we're ready to knock out of the park.

Embrace change; embrace a fun-filled journey.

CONSCIOUSNESS

Wokeness. It's a thing now: to be *woke*, that is. I'm pretty chuffed about it, too. For far too long, there seemed to be a gap in our knowledge & our actions when it came to how we comported ourselves in an ever-growing & ever-churning consumerist society. We learned young that bigger meant better. We were told that the more you have, the more you're worth (not just monetarily speaking). We were also sold the idea that if we wanted to be happy, we needed to not show any cracks. The end result? We're all cracking a bit.

With an incoming tide that is now allowing us to ride to a shore of soft, sandy wokeness—we surfers of sustainability & circular economies are changing how we live, how we buy, what we consume, what we create, how we worship, how we parent, & what we consider love. We're awakening to our impact on the world beyond our own selves & are starting to understand just how potent each & every human being is. All of this is so very overdue, too.

I can remember being a very young child, maybe six years old, thinking about how much trash our little family of four made every week. We had a big dumpster out of the back of our home & while we wouldn't fill it weekly, I'd say we definitely filled it monthly. I remember watching my Dad tie up the ends of thick plastic bags that were almost as big as me. He was strong with big muscles, kinda like He-Man. Still, he lugged the rubbish bags out. They were heavy.

My mind always wondered:
How in the hell did we create so much waste?
Where did it go?
Did everyone else make just as much rubbish?
Why weren't we recycling everything?

My heart & head are heavy thinking through all of this right now & the implications of how much I personally have hurt the earth over the course of my lifetime, simply by throwing shit away. I'd like to pull out the "I didn't know any better!" card, but somewhere even in my little girl mind, I knew what we were doing wasn't right. Trash just didn't evaporate. On the scale of heathen to woke, I'd say I'm still waking. In work & in life I am much more cognizant of how the things I buy & the things I throw away impact the planet & posterity. When working with large organisations, I outright refuse to engage in down-&-dirty retail for products that are made without sustainability, longevity, & a circular economy mindset baked into them.

How can we work towards helping our brands & businesses become woke? First, we need to be aware of our need to awaken. From there, we need a plan. A mindset shift needs to happen: away from money being the be-all & end-all in defining business success. And when we advertise, we need to do so morally & ethically. Yeah, it might take more time & resources up front, & may be challenging at first—but we can literally make the world a better place by thinking consciously when we plan our campaigns & content calendars. Waking up can be confusing, but oh, what a world to inhabit once we're all awake together.

CAKE

Who would I be if I made a list of favourite C-words & didn't even make a nod to the deliciousness that is cake. No matter your sweet, spongy, icing-laden tickle of choice, cake just makes the world go round. In good times & in bad, there's cake. From standard chocolate to funfetti, life is too short not to enjoy & indulge every once in a while. A good life rule: just eat the damn cake. This C-word has nothing to do with marketing or business (unless you run a cake marketing business), but has much to do with balance & blood-sugar, which means it's a-okay with this sweet-toothed tiger.

CURIOSITY MADE
THE CAT

Okay, okay. I know we just went through an entire chapter of my favourite C-words, but it'd be both irresponsible & completely remiss of me not to write an entire chapter on the one word/idea that has gotten me far & into a lot of interesting situations in life to date: curiosity.

From a very young age, curiosity has been my sustaining life-force. It has filled me with an endless supply of passion, adventure, knowledge, fun, empathy, heartbreak, & healing. With an endless amount of the stuff, I've charted waters I didn't even know I didn't know existed. And I'll continue to do so—all thanks to the curious ways in which curiosity helps to keep my head in the clouds & my feet grounded at all times.

Another amazing byproduct of being an unshakeable optimist driven by a need to understand/see/attempt more is that I've become someone who is at home in her own skin. No apologies for who I am, what I stand for, or past mis-steps. With boundless curiosity, one learns early that we can only do our best with what we have. When we know better, we do better. And onwards, onwards, onwards.

Being curious has steeled me, too. Ask anyone who knows me &

they'll tell you that I take no shit, but am grounded in a commitment to empathy & kindness when it comes to others.

Talk about an ambrosial drug, eh?

If curiosity can drive one person to do better in life, just think about what it can do at scale when it comes to work & profession! Wouldn't you know it: when you search "curiosity in business," Google throws quite a lot (ahem, millions) of responses into the fray. While most of the top results feature similarly constructed listicles on just how magical curious leaders & employees are, my curiosity has led me to dive headlong into the idea of CQ: the Curiosity Quotient.

Traditionally, we're assessed as *good fits,* or not, based on IQ. Smarts are a good thing, I'll give you that. In the very near past, a person frequently needed to fit a certain mold of intellectualism to be even considered a certain type of professional success. But we've moved beyond old-school measures of how geekily intelligent a person is based on a standardized tests to measure worth in professional spaces. If EQ tests were all it took to tease out just how successful a leader someone might be, then we'd never have bullies, asshats, & egotistical crackpots at the top of business hierarchies. Yet here we are in a post-GFC world.

On their own, brains do not a complete businessperson make.

Nope, to style yourself an erstwhile complete package (and I'm talking *all that & a bag of Ranch Doritos*), you must be in possession of more than IQ. The sweet spot for impactful & successful humans is that in which intelligence, emotion, passion, & curiosity are more thrown together into a big 'ol mixing bowl & set to bake in the oven. Just as multiple ingredients are necessary for a funfetti cake worth scoffing, so too are multiple skillsets when we're building great business leaders.

So, now that we're all on the same page & know that it takes more than grey-matter to build a rainbow—what's next?

Curiosity, that's what! Even though the concept of a *Curiosity Quotient* has been around for yonks, as an abstract idea when looking beyond the established bounds of how we define intelligence, it's only now being brought into colloquialisms & onboarding procedures in businesses looking for a more well-rounded employee & leadership team.

As a guiding principle for hiring the right kinds of people for any particular business, CQ just makes sense to me. Folded into curiosity are other personality attributes like passion, self-awareness, outside-the-box problem-solving skills, & the ability to keep on keepin' on, even when times are tough. A historically disproportionate focus on IQ, & more recently EQ (emotional quotient), has meant that businesses put head before heart more often than not.

It's not surprising to me that our modern corporations are struggling with employee engagement, a lack of longevity & loyalty to a business, or even high rates of depression & anxiety.

When we tip the scales too far in one direction, something's bound fall over. Business is a balancing act for the human beings who drive the business forward. People who are hungry to learn & grow skills beyond a singular focus learn to employ more sophisticated ways of thinking over time. They also have an increased tolerance for ambiguity.

Both of these things are invaluable assets to businesses. For the most part, though, businesses aren't quite aware of it yet.

The beauty in passion & curiosity is that both of these personality traits ensure that an individual will be a valuable asset to any business for their entire lifetime. This is especially true in the world we inhabit now, where understanding new & evolving digital tools & mastering never before known skillsets is the only way forward.

And hey, don't just take it from me, take it from David Bowie if you're still unconvinced that being a curious wee cat is the best thing you can be! When asked about his artistic nuance & craft, Bowie said: *"What I have is a malevolent curiosity. It's what drives my need to write and what probably leads me to look at things a little askew. I do tend to take a different perspective from most people."*

That different perspective might just be the rocket-fuel needed for creative arts, sciences, & music moving forward.

Ground Control to Major Tom: how do we hone & build up our curiosity quotient, then?
I have a few ideas of just how...

First & foremost, if you are someone who considers yourself strategic, creative, or otherwise cerebral in the way that you approach your work, then you must also find somewhere inside of yourself a blanket permission to be unabashedly curious. You must be intentional in your curiosity. And when people disregard your questions or push aside new ideas or ways of working because they threaten the status quo—then keep digging.

Keep yearning to understand people, cultures, situations, solutions. The more often you allow yourself to be open to the vastness of that which is unknown to you, the more apt you'll be to finding creative solutions to any problem. When I was a freshman in high school, I was put into the senior photography class, in error. Instead of running to the office & asking to be put into a more comfortable environment, I instead looked at the unfamiliarity of my surroundings as a gift. Even then, I knew I was passionate about creating art. I was a complete shit-show when it came to painting or drawing, so photography, music, & the written word were where I threw all of my passion & curiosity.

Unlike wordsmithing or reading music written by other people, photography creatively opened up new worlds & avenues to me from the moment I began learning the rule of thirds. I dove headlong into experimental photography methods, learned to push my own boundaries, & created amazing art. All from making time to be curious.

When you allow your mind to linger on nothing, your mind starts a brilliant dance of unfocussed focus. This dance, when done authentically, builds innovation & iteration. From my background in photography, I evolved with the world around me & learned how to utilize my visual skills across new & emerging digital & social media channels. Over the years, my most strategic career moves—the progression I've lived through—have come thanks to curiosity. As worker bees, we get caught up in the day to day, so my best advice to you is this: allow your curiosity to fuel your creativity at work & you'll never be bored a day in your life.

Data nerds, blue sky thinkers, spreadsheet superheroes unite! We're all so nuanced & have completely individual experiences that make us the professionals that we are. But it's the curious ones amongst us that stand above the rest. Why is this? It's simple, really: those who aim to understand others, those who are curious about causality & creation, are also those who learn to speak different languages of disparate skillsets. When we meld together empathy & a yearning to truly know why things happen as they do, we create marketing magic.

Taking our creativity & applying it through curiosity across skill sets & job types makes us more valuable not only to the companies we work for, but to the world itself. When we start to be genuinely interested in what makes the cogs in the proverbial wheel spin, we start to realize that we are only ever small parts in a much larger whole. Once we accept our smallness, we're able to be bigger than ever.

I know this concept sounds wonky, but hear me out. When we know we're a part of a whole, but not the only part, we then start to find magic in bits & pieces of everyday happenings that we most likely never even noticed before. When we take notice of things, start to ask why, & then make time to ponder new solutions, we take our own journey to another level. My own career has been a study in curiosity more than it has been a straight line from point A to B to C, etc.

When I started in marketing, it was simply to be able to do a job where I could meld together parts of my profession & passion in an artful & creative way. I never thought I'd spend years learning everything from videography, to content production, to social media mastery, to back end digital development, to algorithmic heartbeats, & on then into keynote speaking. But I have done this & then some. Because I am curious about more than just my little corner of the world. I am hell-bent on learning. I am driven to succeed.

I am passionate about teaching others. Curiosity across skillsets is imperative for creating a fulfilling & ever-growing knowledge base in our profession.

We need to be okay with questions.
We must ask questions... keep asking... never stop asking questions.

If there's any gift you can give yourself, take Oprah's advice & make it the gift of time. When it comes to creativity, we must build safe spaces around how we nurture our learning & growth. Sometimes this means literally blocking out time in your calendar for reading, learning, diving into the back end of your website, & crunching some heady numbers. I usually block out an hour each day for myself in which I owe no one anything. I'm not thinking about projects or meetings or board reports. Instead, bookending the day, all I do is dive into something I want to do. I learn what I want to learn. Or I get lost in Mick Jagger's Instagram account for 30 minutes.

Yeah, this happened recently, & I should tell you right now

that Mick's septuagenarian dance moves might light a fire in you that never would've sparked otherwise. If Mick, Keith, & Co. aren't your bag, baby, then simply find something that is & make time to learn. Small bites of entire meals are still nutritious. If you're super keen on acquiring a new skill, then commit to it. Book yourself on a course, join a workshop, or start a group (literally).

Make time to wander in your own head when you're learning. Be kind & gentle with yourself. Listen to death metal if that's what self-kindness looks like. Hell, I'm not gonna judge you. You be you! If you've got a process that you rarely deviate from on a day-to-day basis, add in a step in which you explore other options. Make time, friends. Make damn time for yourself!

COMPASSION AS A COMPETITIVE ADVANTAGE (AND ANOTHER FAVE C-WORD: LAST ONE, I PROMISE!)

W e're facing quite the modern-day dilemma when it comes to building brands while building up the people who work for them. Big businesses come across as faceless, soulless entities driven by greed & the need to stroke the egos of people who sit atop organisational structures.

But the folks who are used to the modern status quo of work-until-you-burn-out-then-keep-on-keeping-on are a dying breed. Literally. Millennials & Gen Z-ers are poised & ready to enter the workforce. Wild-eyed, passionate, ridiculously intelligent, & hungry to make a life that matters. While the old guard might look upon these newbies with scorn & contempt, I for one welcome them as kin.

Why? Because we're starting to see a shift in culture. We're starting to realise that we are more important than any title. In fact, I know of a few companies that now eschew titles completely! If you work hard & you work collaboratively, you're valued. And in the end, we all yearn to be valued while creating value for others.

The one thing that can help you as a marketer & as a professional across any industry, it is this: Kindness.

As Henry James is oft quoted: *"Three things in human life are important: the first is to be kind; the second is to be kind; and the third is to be kind."*

A case in point: a little while ago, I found myself helping to deliver a large project at work. I say "helping" because I was working beyond the scope of my role to lead a group of amazing humans deliver work they were excited about & hungry to undertake. Talk about lucky, right? Yep. For two months, a small group of us toiled, planned, strategized, & laughed together. We worked as a unit, delegating when needed. Working beyond the norm as necessary. Together really is better; we learned this quickly.

Nearing our launch deadline, our small working group grew. Our larger number was pumping on all cylinders—just like that proverbial well-oiled machine we all hear about. Everyone had their tasks & were owning them like the utterly superb professionals they were, & still are. Here's where stress kicked in. With time ticking down, unknowns abounding, & many deliverables on the line to juggle, I could see our group beginning to wobble. At this point, it became my job as a leader to lead with kindness —it was as simple as that.

You see, if you know me at all, you know that I love a hard deadline. Nearing a launch date is akin to the buzz I used to get playing sports. It's like being in 9th inning—you're down by two, you've got runners on second & first, & you're up at the plate—swinging for the back fences, knowing you've got at least three good pitches heading your way. Three good pitches from which to smash a homerun out of the park. I'm almost always confident that a home run is somewhere in the mix. So I watch the pitcher sweat. I grip the bat. And square my hips.

For this project, we got there. We made our deadlines. We made the news. We made the business, our stakeholders, our customers, & (most importantly) ourselves proud. We nailed it! We came together to accomplish something that had never been accomplished at our business before. We did it. Leading confidently matters. Wobbling is okay, wavering isn't. With compassion & kindness leading the way, you tend to lead by doing what's right by the team—not by thyself. Herein lies the magic of compassion as a competitive advantage in business settings.

Why confidence, though? Well, first, why the hell not? Without confidence in ourselves, we have only ripples of worthiness in a wavy sea. As a professional (and as a normal flesh-&-bone-human), I pride myself on my generous spirit of listening. I also pride myself in being able to make final decisions quickly & strategically.

When mixing years of experience & the aforementioned listening, clarity is commonplace in how I work & communicate. Yes, clarity. For me, as for most of us, clarity of purpose & vision equals kindness. Clarity. Equals. Kindness. Hell to the muthafunkin yes it does!

When we're all working hard, the thing that matters most is how we react to others & how we can imbue empathy into our own views & constructive feedback. Vacillating between one idea & another, or changing minds without reason, leaves teams on tenuous & uncertain ground. I love terra firma, a North Star, & a leader who lights the way.

Usually, when we talk about the traits of our favourite leaders, we talk about their vision, their strength, and more often than not, their inherent kindness. But as the flip-side of this same coin, in the day-to-day of modern business culture, being in the trenches means that kindness is very often construed as weakness. The very moment you show your humanity, your individuality, or your imperfections through EQ, you can be labelled as soft, or even worse—weak. I am here to call absolute bullshit on any assertion that puts EQ, empathy, & kindness anywhere on a spectrum that isn't highly skewing towards strong. The strongest, even.

Don't believe me? Let's let science do the talking for a little bit.

There's nothing that gets my knickers in more of a twist than Negative Nellies who think that spreading their doomsday dilemmas & views of the world is the only way to live. These are the souls who love nothing more than to take rose-coloured glasses off positive people like myself, throw them to the ground, & trod upon them. Hoping to break them into a million little pieces. I stand here biting my thumb in the general direction of all you buggers.

Joke's on you, isn't it? Like love, rose-coloured glasses are eternal & there's an endless supply of them available to all of us. Seeing the good in others & being able to persevere in difficult times isn't soft at all. It's just not cutthroat. I mean, yuck. Cutthroat even sounds gross. Don't be that, Team.

Right, to the science bit: on a biochemical level, we feel bloody good when we're kind to other people. This is because we all get a lift in levels of dopamine in the brain when we're nice. Yee haw, here's to getting a natural high from simply being kind.

Another scientifically proven reason for practicing kindness is that it's good for your heart (literally) and slows ageing. Wait... what?!?! The Fountain of Youth exists & kindness be thine name? Sign me up! Yep, acts of kindness are often accompanied by emotional warmth, which means that our bodies produce the hormone oxytocin in the brain and throughout the body.

And we all know what oxytocin does, right? Oxytocin causes the release of a chemical called nitric oxide in our blood vessels, which in turn dilates (expands) the blood vessels. Dilation of blood vessels reduces blood pressure. Yee haw! From this, we can extrapolate out & (mostly) safely say that oxytocin is a "cardioprotective" hormone because it protects the heart. Team, kindness helps our hearts. Swoon.

There's more scientific research out there on the health benefits of being nice to other people—so much research, in fact, that I can't list it all here. So, if you want to know more about it, do what I did & search "Health benefits of being kind" on the Google. I promise you'll be amazed by the amount of research that's been done on the subject.

Never again will I feel bad about doing good. Never again.

WIRED FOR KINDNESS
When it comes down to it, we are all in this adventure of Life together. Our wins, our losses, our heartbreaks, & our pinnacles will be completely individual to us all. But we share a common bond in keeping moving. It is in this bond of acknowledging our collective struggle & triumph that we are able to shine a light on the importance of kindness.

As a species, we are literally wired for kindness. As newborns, we're thrust into a big, wide, fast-paced world. Without the nurturing of our parents &/or main caregivers, we'd never survive. We're the only mammals on earth with a prolonged gestation period & rely on adults to feed, clothe, care for, teach, & evolve us from day one. Like a thread woven into the quilt of life, kindness is rooted deeply in our DNA.

I recently read about a study done in the 1990s by the late Dr.

Masaru Emoto in which a series of experiments was undertaken examining the natural effects of words, prayers, music, & environment on the crystalline structure of water. Sounds a bit, erm, hokey, yeah? But read on. During the study, Dr. Emoto noted that, when kind and loving words were conveyed to water, they formed a complete crystal structure. In comparison, energies of hate & anger didn't (not at the same rate, anyhow). When you think that almost 70% of our body is made up of water, this kind of study makes me think that kindness has a direct impact on our immediate health.

Beyond immediate health & the ability to make water even prettier, kindness is a competitive advantage for leaders. The Zenger Folkman study tracked 51,836 leaders & noted that the most likable leaders who expressed warmth were also the most effective. In simple terms, there's a big difference between leading & managing. To be likable AND effective, you need to be self-aware, empathetic, & able to make decisions that take in more than the bottom line—you need to factor in people first.

So many studies have been done in a similar vein. Kind leaders are not inherently weak. But weak leaders are inherently unkind, untrustworthy, & overrated. As someone who has led many highly engaged teams across professional verticals, I can tell you that the number-one tip to creating engagement in the workplace is trust. From trust comes liking. And from liking comes the ability to gel as a group of individuals. Firing on all cylinders means being there for each other—across good times, bad times, stress, & joy.

The secret to success as far as I see it? Being kind. And not letting any broody, moody storm clouds of human beings tell you any differently.

Also, hugs.
Hugs are always welcome.

TICKING ALL
THE BOXES

A question:
At the setting of the sun, how do you measure whether or not your day has been successful?

A caveat:
Your measures of success don't have to be (perhaps they shouldn't at all be) work-related.

To begin this chapter, I'd like you to ponder on the above. Take all the time you need to answer this one. If you're like me & writing helps you to process your thoughts, write down your answer & keep it somewhere safe to revisit on harder days. I can't recall who first asked me to think through what actual success looked like for me on the micro level. But I am thankful for them asking because years after first asserting a quick, strong answer to the question, my thoughts & beliefs on what success means to me day-in-&-day-out have changed.

Funny that.

I'm curious about you. Did your answer to this question come easily, immediately? Or did it take a while to wrestle with decoupling business measures of success from personal ones?

There's no right or wrong answer, & if you're intrinsically tied to your work, a campaign, your bottom line right now, then so be it. However, I reckon if your answer came fast & is full of work-related nomenclature, there's some digging to be done to uncover a deeper form of understanding around what drives you, why it drives you, & which boxes you're ticking that keep yourself passionate, willing, & able to chase success.

The question above is one that I've asked of every person who has ever interviewed for a role with me. When hiring someone for a role, I try to uncover what it is that drives them. What impassions them. What brings them a sense of accomplishment in moments big, small, & banal. Funnily enough, when put on the spot, a lot of people aren't quite sure how to answer the question of how they define daily success for themselves. In fact, across industries, experience levels, life stages, & confidence levels, I find that the responses I get straight out of the gate are eerily similar.

Most people pepper their answers with marketing measurements. To which I ask folks to dig deeper.
What fills you with a sense of accomplishment beyond work?
What does accomplishment feel like as an emotion?
How do you know you've helped someone?

Yeah, I know. These folks who thought they'd be grilled on their functional skillsets as marketers are getting questions that many of us never take the time to dive into. We know our work inside & out, but we lack intimate knowledge of who we are as people & why we undertake the daily hustle that is a professional job in a fast-paced industry. This leads me to believe that we've all got some unpacking to do around the boxes we're told we must tick to be seen as successful, hardworking, driven individuals. Inside of all of these unseen but omnipresent boxes are standards we didn't write, set by people we don't know. People most likely nothing like us & dead by now. Yet we nurture all their standards & settings regardless, because it's all we know.

We are told from a very young age that being successful, happy & fulfilled looks a certain way. We're given our guardrails, our random rules of engagement, & carry our presumptions (those handed down to us over time by parents, teachers, professors, & bosses) with us everywhere we go in an invisible work bag that gets heavier & heavier with time. When you take a step back & start to look hard at what we're all striving for, the measures are all so seemingly random. They're also defined only by precedence. And if anything is begging to be broken in this life, it's precedence that doesn't fill our souls or lift us as people.

I know, I know. This shit is deep. It should be. We all need to take the time to look beyond our titles & the numbers we deliver to a position description that suits a function in a business machine. We deserve this. When thinking about success & the boxes that have been drummed into me over the course of my lifetime, I can break them down into four distinct areas of my life. Each distinct area is its own nuanced & tightly packed arena—weighted down by expectation, precedence, prudence, & rules that we follow because we aren't taught to question them. Guess what? It's time to start questioning.

Looking into the guts of expectation & success, I've identified FOUR distinct areas of modern life upon which we bear the most weight. Upon opening each box, we find a lot of rules (some unwritten) by which to comport ourselves—but there's more that we uncover than just rules. There are measures of what success is, of individuality, of community, of shame, of failure, of success, of kindness, of empathy, of silence, & of how we should walk through the world. In essence, as we grow up & grow into adulthood, we stop growing—we get smaller, to be able to fit in boxes.

THE FOUR LIFE BOXES:

The Work Box

As a marketer, the work box is obviously the first one that I'm going to rip open. Titles, pay checks, organizational echelons, working for the "dream company" —what the heck are we chasing anymore, folks? All of it? None of it? When I was a little girl, I had two dreams about the kind of work I wanted to do when I grew up. The first job was simple: I wanted to be a marine biologist. I wanted to be on the ocean more often than not. And I wanted to help keep the planet happy & healthy. I wanted to make a difference & leave the world a better place than I'd found it. Such a good Girl Scout, aye? Over time, I was told that marine biology might be something that wasn't as important as being a lawyer, or a doctor, or any professional that came with titles & lots of dosh. I was young, I was impressionable, I was female (ahem, I still am female); I set this dream aside.

The second dream I had was something I completely threw myself into from a very young age, so please do not laugh at it. I mean, chuckle away in private if you wish, but don't do it to my face—I might ninja kick you in the knee. Hi-ya! So yeah, the truth. My biggest professional dream as a little girl in rural Southern California was to be the tambourine player in Elton John's touring band. Not *a* tambourine player, *the* tambourine player. Can you even imagine the fun, the rock n roll, the rhythm in such a job?!?! Yeah, me neither. Fuuuuuuuun!!!

I should back up a bit & give you a bit more context. Something you might not know about me, unless we're close friends or family, is that I am quite possibly Sir Elton John's biggest fan. Bold claim—yeah, I know it is. Come at me, super fans. Pen to paper, forever in ink on paper. Over the course of the past 21 years, I have seen Sir Elton & his band perform 21 times, & the last time I saw him in concert was a life-changer. Literally. I not only had a front-row view of my musical hero, but my wife & I actually got to be ON THE GODDAMN FUCKING STAGE with Elton as he rocked n rolled to "Saturday Night's Alright For

Fighting" at a concert in Las Vegas at Caesar's Palace.

But, as I'm sure you've cottoned on to by now, I wouldn't be writing this book on marketing & marketers if I had actually become Elton's tambourine 2IC. Instead, I learned to play clarinet, then moved on to piano—& then, as a young adult, realised that the music industry was a hard place for a woman to survive in back then (& might still be). So I gave up the dream & the ghost.

Not because something might be too hard, but because I was also told consistently that I needed to get a *real job*. What the actual fuck is a real job? The only thing in my life that I'd do differently, if I could do anything over, would be putting aside my musical dreams early on. But hey, I did, so now with the gift of experience & time, I won't allow this to happen again.

Because I allowed the idea of what being a professional meant, looked like, & should be to permeate into my mind, I gave up on my childhood dreams. As I've aged & as I've climbed the proverbial ladders in the marketing world, I've dug deep to not allow the expectations of others to dictate my happiness or how I define success at work. Simply put, if I'm helping someone, I'm succeeding. The titles, the dream jobs, the money— none of it matters unless you do something that does. In a profession that puts so much onus on individuality & creativity, we sure are adept at playing by the rules.

Be good at what you do – but not too good.
Be individual – but don't be quirky.
Win awards – but don't be proud of them.
Work as a team – but make sure you shine.
When you shine – don't shine too brightly.

The rules are there. Whether you've seen them laid out in front of you in completely literal ways or know them as a big lump in your throat or weight on your chest, they're there. It is my extreme hope that all of us stop placing the expectations of others in our own work boxes. You don't have to tick of anything anyone else does to be successful at doing what you do. Small moments of joy, curiosity, wonder, & giving make us marketers some of the luckiest professionals on the planet. But until we stop trying to stroke the egos of people playing finite games in an infinite arena, we'll never be fulfilled. Tick all of the bloody boxes as you want as defined by others—they won't bring you joy.

Instead, define your own success. Build your own landscape for how a life well lived & work well done look. The sooner you do this, the sooner you will find true success when it comes to your work.

The Creativity Box

Ah, the old creativity box. Something we all have to tick at some point in our lives. Regardless of whether you're at the Excel-guru end of the problem-solving spectrum or you're dancing with your head in the clouds with nary a tether back to reality, we're all creative humans. The reason you're alive & reading this sentence is because you've had to be bloody creative throughout your life, figuring out how to simply make it through your days alive. You've had to overcome obstacles. Hell, you've had to be a creative wizard to simply exist. So, before I go any further please say this with me: "I am a freaking creative wizard. I am a magical unicorn of a human. I AM CREATIVE." (SAY IT!)

Right, back to ticking the creativity boxes & unpacking them as we go. Over the course of many years, I've learned how to spot a creative. You know what they look like, right? We all do —we've been told over, & over, & over that to be creative you have to look a certain way. You have to think a certain way. You have to live a certain way. And by "certain way," I mean differently to the rest of the crowd. Different to professional marketing norms of management & strategy. What do I mean by this? Basically, you have to wear all black. You're a ninja. You also have to not wash your hair for days—maybe weeks! You need to be able to glide from Smurfs to Sassafrass Street in San Diego & make everything make sense when pitching to clients. Basically, you're a nutter. A socially accepted one, but a nutter nonetheless.

LOL, jokes. Truth bomb time. I fit into zero stereotypes when it comes to creativity. This is simply because I refuse to label myself as such. I've played the games where I've straightened my hair, dressed like the other ladies of the upper marketing royalty, & have spoken in the tongues of data nerds. But just because I also have a love for data, spreadsheets, & strategy does not mean I am not creative.

When I started my career in marketing, I simply wanted to be able to collect a regular paycheck for doing something that even remotely looked & felt like storytelling. In the days before social & digital media (yes, I was alive in the dinosaur days, my young friends), I spent a lot of time writing advertorial copy, creating longform articles for sponsored sections in magazines, & I dabbled in my beloved passion of photography. I also quickly started learning the rules of engagement in the marketing game.

About five years into my career, I was bored. I'd done every kind of traditional advertising & I was tired down to my soul writing about business goals & geothermal mud pools. I needed something exciting to spin my wheels. I yearned for a challenge. I won't lie, there were moments (many, many moments) where I thought about running away to join Elton John & play tambourine near the front of stage until he decided I was worthy of being part of the band. I didn't run away, though. I was a young mother, a wife, & and was just putting roots down in New Zealand—pretty darn far from home in California. So I stayed. I also went out searching for something else to do.

As much as I'd like to say that I found digital & social media marketing, the truth is that they found me. Along with this finding, of sorts, also came passion for work that was yet undefined, unrefined, & mostly undiscovered. I threw myself into every aspect of online & digital. I learned not only how to build websites, but how to fill them. I learned not only how to set up online communities, but how to build them. I took pay cuts to jump into roles that I was able to write & define. All for the sake of curiosity & creativity.

In the uncharted territories of the online world I got to know the best & worst of society all at once. I was able to become a connector, a content creator, a producer, an editor, & a publisher all at once. I was (ahem, & still am) a freaking creative powerhouse. Why? Because I have always fostered creativity above anything else in my box-ticking life. There are moments when my soul actually feels heavier than normal. Kinda like when you drop your big towel in the bathtub by accident & it's sopping wet, I often have to step back & wring everything out before finding my creative groove again. Without creativity, there's nothing. Tick the box, but for chrissakes, do it on your own terms.

The Family/Friends Box

Our family & friends are a sum total of how we see, experience, & understand the world around us. The people we love most influence us most. They are our biggest supporters, but they can also be the people who most hold us back. By carrying the weight of our own expectations & then piling on top those of the people we care for most in the world, we learn to quiet curious whispers from deep within that push us to find joy in the mundane, that tell us to dance on tables, that remind us to follow our hearts—not rules made for us by people who never knew us.

From the moment we're born, we're inundated with the rules,

desires, & dreams (lived out or yet unfulfilled) of others. Our neuroses are passed down from generation to generation. We believe that we must unquestioningly follow the paths forged behind us. We hold tight to childhoods constrained by societal norms that we were not part of creating.

When we're little, we're free & curious. We're born perfectly incapable of anything other than delighting in the moment we're in. But as we age, we're taught to reign in our curiosity, to hide our joy, & to stop playing for the sake of playing. Good god, even as someone else's mom, I love playing for the sake of playing! When we leave home, or begin the branching out, we start to meet *our people.* These people are family by choice. They are spirits that know our spirits. They are either so much like us or so much not like us that we find comfort in knowing we have a community.

Friends. Thank god for friends. Also, FUCK YOU, FRIENDS!

What usually comes with our communities—whether we share a genetic bloodline or not—are expectations & unwritten laws. Sometimes these expectations & unwritten laws go unspoken. Even so, they hover just above us. Always there. Always guiding us. Always reminding us about what's right & what's wrong. Telling us to sit up a bit straighter, to take up less space, to make more space, to hurry up, to slow down, to one-up everyone else, to be humble. Reminders constantly reminding us to remind others of the reminders to fit into the goddamn box that's been assigned to you. Because that is exactly what we do. That is how life is done. If we veer too far off charted paths, even liberal hippy-child paths, we lose at life. Understand?

I understood for 35 years. Then I started to shake off the reminders. To set my "friends & family expectations" notification to silent & to fuck shit up a bit—so to speak. You see, when I was a little girl, I was told I could be anything I wanted to be. I was encouraged to chase my wildest dreams. The wildest ones!

But only so far. Remember, there are always boundaries & guard-rails when it comes to box-ticking exercises in life. While I was a very happy child, a freewheeling, BMX riding, Sporty Spice of a tomgirl, from about age 8yrs old I put little Cassie away. I wished her well, locked her in a deep dark closet, & brought out the good girl I knew everyone wanted.

When you're a kid, especially a female kiddo who might just grow up to be something other than the norm, you become super accustomed to spotting platitudes. Platitudes are one thing, they're manageable. The actual fear of not meeting the expectations of those around you by calling out the bullshit is something else completely. My family loved me like every kid dreams of being loved—they still do. Better, harder, & more openly than you can imagine. The same goes for my friends. But I heard the deafening din of rules unspoken. I carried the weight of expectations. I learned to tick boxes. For a long, long time, life was heavy. It's not anymore.

When we bend to familial & societal pressures, we lose pieces of ourselves. If you're like me, you have a few out-there people in your life who remind you that being out there is probably the best way to be at all times. They whisper in your ear, "Awe, go on, Cass. Take your tambourine to the next Elton concert... you may just get on stage!" They help you feel invincible even when you're crumbling. Ticking boxes when the ticking becomes a pleasurable experience in freedom is one thing. Ticking them when you feel constrained is another.

My best advice when it comes to family & friends is this: follow your own arrow. You're the protagonist in your own life. You're the person who gets to decide the direction of your profession, the direction of your path. If you want to be a copywriter, be a copywriter. If you don't want to be an Excel wizard & hate Gantt Charts as much as me, eschew the wizardry. You're allowed to hoe your own damn row. Your friends & family? They'll be there regardless.

Sometimes, boxes aren't worth ticking if it means giving up important parts of who you are. Your true friends & your community beyond will show themselves by filling the boxes you need to tick with lightness, kindness, & hope. Always follow the ones who fill you up over those who weigh you down.

The Spiritual Box
I've tried to meditate more times than I can count on both hands & feet, & just don't get it. Sitting still never has been & never will be my forte. As a teenager, my friends nicknamed me *Wigglebutt* simply because they never saw me in any state other than in motion. To this day, I don't find joy, peace, or calmness in sitting in silence. My ass starts to hurt, my knees squeak, & I end up focusing on the length of time left until I'm once again free to wiggle my damn butt. Ticking ye olde spiritual box is the cool thing to do right now.

I can't tell you how often I've heard friends, celebrities, colleagues, influencers—all kind of people—talking about how much they love their transcendental meditation. Their hot yoga. Their avocado-kale-spirulina smoothie bowl with acai. Their week-long screen detox in Bali with a private vegan chef. All in the name of cleansing thyself & maybe even feeling a bit superior to others when it comes to spirituality. What the actual sheezy? Can we just not? If you really love your smoothies, your hot yoga, & your Head Space App, that's awesome—but undertaking all of these things & bragging about them on Monday in WIPs isn't going to make you a more woke human being.

Let me tell you, friends, it's not your Lululemons at lunchtime or your quinoa poke bowls delivered by Uber Eats that will breed a consciousness at scale for humanity. The simple idea that will change the world, though? It's understanding that we all do spirituality our own way. Call it religion, creed, belief systems, or a feeling of oneness with everything—spirituality isn't a game where we keep score. It's painfully personal & as beauti-

155

fully big as we each want to make it in our lives.

For me, spirituality comes in many forms & in moments that I couldn't plan for in a million years. From the time I was a very young girl, my earliest memories, in fact, I remember finding absolute peace in nature. The green moss that grew between the paved road & the dirt hill that lead up to the back door at my grandmother's house dazzled me. I found religion in the quiet moments before dawn watching my grandfather fastidiously tie his heavy black leather shoes before he'd take my hand & walk me down the path to pump water for the cattle from the well.

As I aged, it became easier to spot moments of oneness & transcendence in mundane, banal moments—moments that have etched themselves into my mind as the most beautiful times of connection a human might ever have felt. Sundown near the Pacific—slightly sunburnt after a day playing in the waves at Silver Strand Beach on Coronado Island. Running through fields of corn with my cousin Ashlee as pinks & purples painted the skies above us, just before the day said hello to the night. When I left the United States & moved to New Zealand, I carried spirituality with me in familiar, happy things. In music, in knowing how to read the tide & the break of the waves, in open-hearted laughter from the people around me. I didn't need to tick a damn box to feel awake. To be truly conscious.

As we get older & fall more into line with how we should be living & working, we tend to lose ourselves. All of us do. And whether we accept the loss of who we are or fight like hell to regain our potency, we all know there's something bigger, something connecting us all. We've left our spiritual gardens unattended for so long that we're thirsting for anything that will quiet our minds for even a short moment. In the marketing trade, a good way to forget about the weeds invading our spiritual gardens is to work more, to assign our self-worth as being interconnected with our titles & pay packets.

Why do we do this? Why do we nourish other people's box-ticking exercises when it comes to spirituality? Why do we sharpen our pencils in hopes of seeing each box filled with a giant X or tick? What if we smashed the boxes, broke the mould, & decided to re-write the rules?

For me, this has meant I listen to the inner voice in me that says I am competent, I am individual, & I get to make my rules when it comes to how I'll engage at work. This isn't selfish. Well, yeah, it kind of is. But I'm cool with it because it's selfishness that lifts the whole self. Not the title. Not the tenuous hold of ego. Feeding our spirits is the best reason to take time to tend our gardens. Find your consciousness, release who you are, & you'll find your work & personal life become what they've always been: one & the same.

Now that we've taken a deep dive into the boxes we all tick —whether we want to or not—I wonder why we keep passing down such flawed ideas of a life well lived from generation to generation. Along the way, we add in our own fears & insecurities while constructing new boxes. Piling fear higher & deeper than it was for us.

Just imagine what would happen if we threw everything we thought we knew to the wind.
We'd find BALANCE.
We'd find WONDER.
We'd find CHALLENGE.
We'd find OURSELVES.

Before you start another day, another campaign, another project, another job, ask yourself: which boxes am I ticking today... and do I need to?

WORK FOR NO ONE

When I was little, I never had a strong idea about what I wanted to be when I grew up—other than fulfilled & free. I didn't dream about a white wedding, & I definitely wasn't going to have kids before the age of 40. My dreams consisted of being around people & creating. I knew that I needed to tell stories. Be it on film, through words, or via a melody, stories were everywhere, which meant, for me anyhow, magic was everywhere too.

I didn't envision my future self working in an office for someone I'd never met before. Clock watching. Filing reports & shuffling paper to an end that really didn't justify the means at all & might never. Some days would be better than others; sure they would. I'm an unshakeable optimist—I can find the beauty in any weed popping through a crack in the sidewalk. But sheesh, over time I really lost my vision of where I not only wanted to be, but where I needed to be as well.

Little Cassie never would've thought that grown-up Cassie would choose a life where freedom wasn't really all that free. Where the whim of others would be an already faded North Star of sorts. But that's exactly what happened as I started down the path of becoming a marketing professional. Because professional life encompasses much more than the work we do & the things we produce, I started to look for people to work for that

I could admire & learn from. Richard Branson, Sheryl Sandberg, Phil Knight, Walt Disney, Oprah! The list I made in my own head of women & men who inspired me & countless others were the bar for managers & bosses I sought out in my own life.

Oh, how fast the mighty fall. Time & time again, I was thrown together with managers who weren't leaders. My heart broke so many times. So. Many. Times. For so long, I believed that it was the good eggs who made it into leadership positions; more often than not, though, it was the rotten ones. As a young professional, I felt powerless to do anything for fear of reprisal & outright firing. I learned very fast that the accepted rules of engagement in certain corporate settings might not match your own or even fit within the bounds of your own moral compass. But that didn't matter: you either played by the rules or you were kicked off the team. Stink.

When I was in my late 20's, I started working as a marketing manager in the promotions, events, & tourism space in a small seaside town on Auckland's North Shore called Takapuna. From the day I first set foot in New Zealand to the present day, Takapuna has always been a happy place swirling with So-Cal vibes & spiritual connections.

When I started the aforementioned job, I was a young mother, hungry to make a difference in the world for myself—but mostly for my toddler daughter. I've always wanted to leave the world a better place for her. To say I was bright-eyed & bushy-tailed in getting a job so near the ocean & with the promise of creativity & strategic thinking would be an understatement.

In all reality, I was stoked to be moving into a creative-*ish* role, promoting the amazing things our local community had to offer. My first day in the office, I found a parking spot right near the ocean & had to pinch myself. How lucky was I to be in a place where I could hear the waves crashing as I ordered my morning coffee & to have a beautiful beach close enough for lunchtime swims & after work jogs. Lucky. Man, I was so thankful on day one.

Then came day two. <Insert the sound of a speeding car screeching to a stop>

Arriving at work on day two was very similar to day one, except the façade of kindness that my hiring manager wore in the interviews we shared together & on the first day of working together was gone. I walked into the office, smiling from ear to ear, only to watch as my new boss dressed two of my colleagues down in a way that was both humiliating & hurtful. My gut sank. My mind said, "Well, shit. This isn't going to get any better, is it?" Both gut & mind were correct.

This woman, the job, & a culture of corporate bullying meant that the next twelve months of my life were both the most harrowing & the most horrific. As much as we try separate work & home life, the cold, hard truth of any job in any sector is that we have but one life. You do not become a different person & live on a different plane of existence when you cross the threshold of your office. You're you. At all times, you might not bring all of who you are, think, & feel to your work, for fear of reprisal or judgement—but who we are is always underneath the ways in which we self-silence . We are always a full picture. We just learn very, very early on how to crop said picture to suit different environments.

During the twelve months I worked in this early job, I suffered from a lot of mental anguish. I learned to doubt myself & others. I went into survival mode without ever having a chance to change gears into a thriving state of working. At one point I can remember sitting on the floor of my office after hours, weeping into an 8-page, double-sided, 8pt font printed spreadsheet. At the time, I had a very ill 2yr old child at home & I was desperate to be with her.

Looking back on it now, I should've told my manager to get

stuffed. Family before work. Always. But I was young & desperately needed my paycheck to pay for basics. So when my manager walked into my office around 4:59pm & sneered at me, "I've gone through this document with a fine-toothed comb & there are two spelling mistakes—now it's your turn to find them before you can leave," I lost my will to want to work. I also almost lost my will to live.

Bully cultures suck ass. Yet they still exist. And, in marketing—let's talk openly here—they're rife. I've never known a cattier kind of culture than that of the creative type in all of my years working. I should point out that I have worked in some absolutely loving, collaborative, & engaged teams over the years—but there's always one. And it only takes one to upset the entire group, right? Why is it that we allow this to happen? Are we all little kids who had their LEGO house smashed & have yet to get over it? I don't know the answers to those questions, but I do know that there's a lot of work to do in our industry to help lift each other. There's so much we need to work through to showcase the work of collaborative, empathetic, kind teams over the cultures that spawn a downward spirals & inward implosions of team members.

To finish the above story, I never found both of the spelling mistakes in the 2,000+ word document that I was supposed to be checking over. And at about 8pm that night, as the snarling assassin laughed over me while I cried, I called it a day. I told this wimpy, power-hungry wannabe that I was going home to be with my family. She could get fucked looking for her two misspelled words. As I grabbed my things to leave, this woman had the gall to turn to me & say, "Actually, the words weren't misspelled. They're just spelled differently by different people.

You wrote the word 'program' but I prefer the posher-looking 'programme' instead." HASHTAGE RAGE! This meanness inherent in the woman I was working for made me promise to me— I would never, ever again work *for* someone. I would only ever work *with* others. Never would I allow another weaker, meaner, assholish-to-the-core human to dictate my self-worth through disapproval. Fuck that.

Language matters. Dear lord, it matters. The stories we tell ourselves & the voices in our own heads are brought to life by the words we use to associate ourselves & our value when we attribute our worth. We are all worthy. We are all allowed to tell someone who harms us in any way at work to fuck right off. Even if you're not a big fan of expletives, make sure you become a fan of strong-enough language to remind yourself of your superpowers. You never need to work for someone ever again. Working with people is a choice we all get to make & to be very discerning about.

Case in point. After working for some time (a few years) in a business whose moral standards increasingly did not match my own, I handed in my resignation without already having another job to go to. Before making my mental shift away from working for others to adding value by working alongside them, I wasn't even the slightest bit nervous or frightened. There wasn't a door closing behind me; on the contrary, a world of opportunities was opening up just in front of me.

I only needed to open my eyes to see them. I only needed to open my heart to know them. Also, it'd be bad of me not to mention that I was pretty excited to leave big corporate life behind. If this wasn't the big kick in the ass to FINALLY start my own business, I didn't know what was. Choosing to walk away was choosing to pay tribute to the younger version of myself who wept on the floor of that office searching for a non-existent needle in an Excel spreadsheet haystack. Young Cassie deserved better & older Cassie was going to honour her by doing better for them both.

When it comes down to hierarchies, structures, slow moving

ships, speedy tribes, or any way of working, always remember this: you get to choose how you engage or don't. You are the captain of your own ship. Don't rely on a business, a person, or anyone other than yourself to find your North Star. It's up to you to look up into the night sky & chart a course towards your goals & aspirations.

My best advice for a long, happy career is: don't work for anyone.

By rights, work with everyone.

FEED THE FEED/
SELLING OUR SOULS
TO THE SCROLL

About two months ago, my wife found me wandering around aimlessly in our front lounge, muttering to myself. This isn't to say that I don't often wander aimlessly & mutter to myself; I do. In fact, I pride myself on my ability to shut off from the world every once in a while & dive deep into reckons & thoughts to which I haven't yet given any oxygen. This time was different, though. Once she'd stopped the muttering & had me back in the land-of-now, she told me I looked as if I was in some kind of a trance. She was wholly convinced that I'd either had quite the breakthrough or started on the path to one helluva breakdown—maybe both at the same time.

The good news was that I wasn't unravelling. The bad news was, yes, I had had quite the breakthrough.
When it came down to it, in the moment, I had to laugh for fear of crying when I told her what I'd been saying on repeat:

DEAR LORD, SOMEONE SOMEWHERE PLEASE TAKE MY PHONE AWAY FROM ME!
DEAR LORD, SOMEONE SOMEWHERE PLEASE TAKE MY PHONE

AWAY FROM ME!
DEAR LORD, SOMEONE SOMEWHERE PLEASE TAKE MY PHONE
AWAY FROM ME!
DEAR LORD, SOMEONE SOMEWHERE PLEASE TAKE MY PHONE
AWAY FROM ME!
DEAR LORD, SOMEONE SOMEWHERE PLEASE TAKE MY PHONE
AWAY FROM ME!

Thankfully, my wife took my phone from me. She walked the little sucker all the way to the back room of our house & tucked it away in a drawer for safekeeping until I could explain to her in more detail the *why* behind my morning of mayhem. Going back in time to a pre-muttering reality, I'd been attempting to start a work project. In fact, for hours & hours on end, I'd been looking up information, doing my due diligence from a data perspective, & spent countless moments trawling the inter-webs looking for more content to fill both my mind & the strategy I was about to put forward.

The strategy & the project weren't small bananas day-to-day work in progress. This was the fun stuff. This was a project that needed to meld data, insight, research & creativity. And we all know what we need to pull all these things together in a way that makes sense to everyone else, right? Yep: time.

So, as all mad scientist marketers do, I built time into my days by waking up at the sparrow's fart (3 am) each morning for two weeks. You'd think I'd have cracked this project over the course of two weeks of clear time in the mornings, but I hadn't even made a dent. This was the most frustrating process of my life. I just couldn't get over a seemingly insurmountable speed bump of melding magic & mastery. I had lots of information, but that elusive last piece that finished the puzzle was still, well, elusive. I couldn't find the little bugger. And on the morning of the muttering, I finally realized why I couldn't reach the end. Every time my mind started to wander into a creative territory, I balked. Instead of doing the hard yakka, instead of wrestling with the

165

problem & rumbling with it, I would pick up my phone, open one (or more) social media platforms, & then mindlessly scroll.

WTAF.

When I'd get lost in Mick Jagger's Instagram newsfeed for an hour, I'd lose precious time & concentration. My phone was a slippery slope on a hiding to nothing. And I was blind to the impact that my mindless scrolling & purposeful procrastination had on me finishing the work I needed to get done. Here began the wandering, the pondering, the muttering. What I needed was an intervention.

I needed someone to hide my goddamn phone from me. To throw it out the window from the 100th floor (while checking for pedestrians below, obvs; I didn't want anyone injured). To toss it overboard into the sea. Fuck this digital addiction shit. My iPhone could go for a swim with the fishes & I wouldn't flinch at this point.

Seriously, though, at this point in time, I felt absolutely helpless. My brain wasn't happy with my hands. I had to admit right there & then that I was an addict. I was addicted to screens & to scrolling. My brain needed the dopamine hit of a like, comment, or share. Ohhhhhh, look! Another little double-tapped heart. Fun! It beggars disbelief that I didn't see this sooner: all of the signs were there. I needed rest. My hands needed to work. My mind needed to ponder deeply without distraction. And my soul needed filling of another type. So, there & then, I changed gears for the better. While it may seem a bit OTT, I left my phone in the back drawer where my wife put it for the rest of the morning. On the way to work that day, I then took all social media apps off my phone. I won't lie to you, I've been working in social media for yonks now. I know the science behind our addiction to the platforms. I've intimately used the rules of addiction to fuel content that drives more checking back. More scrolling. Yuck. Cass, what in the world possessed you?

Anyhow, I'm now two months clean. No social media on my phone, & I've found that (whilst I definitely went through withdrawal symptoms) not having social media on my phone has done nothing to hurt my actual social life. I repeat: not having social media on my phone *has not* impacted my actual, real, in the world social life at all. What it's done is the opposite! I now have more time each day to write, to ponder, to work, to play with my daughter. Taking apps off of my phone that are built to specifically hook us & keep us on a platform as long as possible has lifted my ability to think & create by freeing my mind to wander.

When apple updated their iOS to include a weekly "screen time" reminder, I was horrified. This update happened just before my morning of mutters, & completely makes everything that happened afterwards make sense. The first weekly update I got horrified me. I was spending over four hours a day on my phone. FOUR HOURS A DAY & SOME CHANGE. Whoa. The thing that floored me was that I couldn't remember any of those four hours. What in the world was I ingesting? Why was I staring at a screen, simply to mindlessly watch other people's lives fly past me at the speed of a throw-away comment or like? When I recently looked at the numbers, I was more saddened than shocked. Most of us are spending between 4 & 8 hours a day on our phones. The majority of that time is not productive time, either. Our lives, now tethered intrinsically to our devices, are being chewed up by mindlessness. This has got to change.

In our home, we're combatting smartphone & screen-time overuse in the most old fashioned of ways: we're leaving our phones in another room & spending time together making memories. We play a lot of card games, we draw, we talk about things that are happening in the world, & we let our creative spirits come out to play in ways we never made time for before. You never truly know the joy of motherhood until you have a sing-along with your kid in the front room on a Friday night to songs you're making up on the spot. Watching my daughter's eyes light up when a silly rhyme slides out of my mouth is pure joy. It's more addictive than selling my soul to any newsfeed.

As professional marketers, I think it's time we're all more intentional about how we use social & digital media as people, & as those putting more & more of a glut of content out into the world. It is on us, not the platforms themselves, to do better by & for the communities we serve. Here are some of my favourite tips for stopping the mindlessness that is scrolling timelines & newsfeeds.

Be hyper-vigilant & super intentional when it comes to your attention

Don't just be intentional; throw a cape over your shoulders & be SUPER intentional with who & where you spend your time & attention. Social media & most digital interfaces today are built to take advantage of our biology. To keep our attention piqued, platform designers spend their entire working lives trying to hack our own human algorithms—pumping our brains full of all kinds of chemicals that tell us mindless scrolling is an action that should be rewarded.

Personally, I'll admit right here & now that there have been times when I've found it pretty hard to focus my attention on something when I have my phone anywhere within eyesight or notifications turned to "on" on my computer. To counter my own lack of intestinal fortitude when it comes to ignoring the siren call of my devices, I try to put my phone in a place where I am not (e.g., out of the room). I also quite often disconnect from Wi-Fi or switch on airplane mode.

Without incoming notifications or distractions on demand, it's much easier to dive headlong into a problem & find a creative solution. Focus is the key to completing any & all tasks, but our handheld devices are built to do the opposite. They're built to keep us entertained, engaged, & online. If you have a little niggle in your tummy that tells you there might just be a little issue with how much time you're spending online or that you're unable to focus, now might be the time to cut the proverbial cord & go back to the good 'ol days of offline pondering & pontification.

The most impactful thing you'll ever do is to practice self-awareness when it comes to yourself & the time you while away on devices. If we are all intentional in the practice of protecting our time & attention, we'll be able to accomplish just about anything.

Take the apps that drain the most of your time off your phone
Taking all of the social media apps off my phone almost caused me a mini-anxiety attack when I first did it. Why? Because I am tethered to them. I feel both a strange mix of FOMO (fear of missing out) & JOMO (joy of missing out) when I'm on scroll street. There's something in the shiny apps with their little red alerts telling me someone, somewhere wants to connect with me on something deep or inane.

In reality, though, 99% of the time, social media apps are anything but social. They're a mix of banal advertising, fake realities, & negativity overload. Mindlessly scrolling dials up unawareness. We become numb to the fact that the people behind the Photoshopped smiles & silly videos are hurting just as much as we are. We lose touch with humanity. As marketers & as keepers of brand stories, it's our job to lead by example. Like parenting, doing the hard stuff means we have to give up a bit of our own pleasure. But the better we act & interact online as brands & as representatives of particular products, the better we build up the fortitude needed in others to comport themselves in the same way.

After taking social media & other apps that drain time off my phone, I found that I was able to hop onto a channel sporadically, then hop off. No guilt. No FOMO. I won't lie to you: the urge to tap into another universe is strong. Especially when I feel impassioned about something going on in the real world.

If you can't go app-less on your phone, or you're prone to aimless scrolling on your desktop—fear not! A good way to get out of the habit of scrolling is to set yourself a time limit. I try to scroll for no more than 15 minutes at a time before getting back on track & focussing on more productive pursuits during the day (or night). You might need 30 minutes of mindless online socialising to calm your brain a bit—the important thing is to set yourself a realistic limit so that you're not heading online for a single Google search, & then looking up to realise you've spent ten hours reading through the entire history of the Vikings when they landed in England. Tough cookies, though, them Vikings. And remember that while going cold turkey is one way to get more of you back into your days, it's not the only way. You do you, Boo. Do what makes you feel good.

Notice what makes you feel good
This is so, so, so important. SUPER important, even. Being present & understanding your gut feelings when you're online is something a lot of us don't do well, myself included. Beyond the time we spend online, there's an emotional & mental toll taken on us. We may passively scroll, but our hearts & minds are still set to "on" when we're looking at how goddamn perfect everyone else's lives are when shared through the lens of algorithmically curated optimism.

Multiple scientific studies have concluded beyond the shadow of any doubt that even the "good stuff" on social media can make us feel like shit. That's right, we're hardwired for truth, & if all we see is rainbow & butterflies, then we begin to misconstrue our moments of hardship & toil as being akin to failure. We can change the way social media & online content streams make us feel by changing who we follow, how we interact (or don't) with content, & by simply being attuned to our own inner voices.

The first & most important part of changing the way you surf the net & create waves for others to ride is in being BFFs with your gut. You might think that you need to follow Beyoncé because she's an ass-kicking, fierce, feminist legend—but maybe seeing her stories of strength only make you feel weak. You know what you do, then? You unfollow Beyoncé. WHAAAT?!?! Yeah, I know. This is akin to social media sacrilege. But if you're feeling anything other than lifted or fulfilled by anyone else's posts, you need to unfollow. You must turn off the tap. Turn down the noise. Anyway, I'm sure Bey will understand your reasons for needing to build your own self esteem before you continue building hers.

Being cognisant of what you put out into the world means you know the emotions you are feeling in the moment & can call them by name. Once you start to understand what makes you feel good, bad, or otherwise, you can curate your social feeds to suit more positive interactions. Just because you're supposed to love Beyoncé & follow kale-eating macro health bloggers doesn't mean you have to, if following them makes you feel a little bit less than awesome. It's totally okay to unfollow or never follow the crowd in the first place. Take note of the good stuff, take note of the bad. Build inwards or outwards based on your knowing.

Make play a priority
Last weekend, my wife & I went to visit with friends for an evening of wine, laughter, & games. The four of us adults are quite often on our phones (as is made obvious by our Insta stories & Tweet threads), so I was actually a bit anxious before heading over for the evening. Why the anxiety? Well, I guess in my heart of hearts, I was hoping that all of us would somehow magically forget our phones & that we'd have a night to remember

filled with stories, memories, & a bit of mayhem to boot. As we arrived at our friends' house, I noticed something magical on their table—no, it wasn't the mezze platter that looked more inviting than anything I'd seen in years—it was a stack of cards & a new game I'd not yet heard of before. As we greeted each other, smooched cheeks, & poured the wine, my anxiety was set to ease. Not a single phone came out over the course of the evening.

We finished off a few bottles of red wine, told stories, laughed our asses off, & played cards until well into the small hours. By making play a priority—even as adults (especially as adults) — we bonded. I can recall the hilarious details of our game-play, I can sing back to you the music that played on their radio, & I now know where to go when we need another night of fun & play.

At work, I've started to make play a priority as well. By turning strategy sessions into moments for expression & riffing together as a team, I find our outputs are multiplied exponentially. Simply turning one's phone upside down on the table doesn't stop an influx of distracting notifications & disruptions in meetings.

When we make focus & play a priority in the office, we quickly learn about each other & we learn how to work with our strengths to build alpha teams who not only work well together, but who trust each other. When you bring outcome & trust into the workplace, you get from this a high-performance culture. Today more than ever, it is important to make time to play! Play!

Read more books with actual pages
Whoa. What? Yeah, I know, right? Books with pages. You're reading one right now. Huzzah! Not only do they look positively beautiful stacked in corners & lined up in bookshelves,

they're also good for your brain—& your soul. Books are my Bae these days (sorry Wifey, love you & your pages—just differently). Books are beautiful. They hold wonders of every world imaginable. They also don't have notifications, in-built distractions, or require ad-blockers to keep shit you're not interested in from stealing your concentration away. Books are magical. If you're like me & have a multitude of mechanical pencils & highlighters within reach, then you have the added joy of being able to write in them!

There's also tactile pleasures to behold as you hold your actual book with actual pages. You get to touch each page as you turn it. There's so much joy in a turning page—I recommend pages to endless scrolling. But hey, this is just me. If you like to read your books on an e-reader, that's just fine & dandy as well. I'm not judging you! That said, our unsung heroes of modernity are the throw-backs, the wonder-filled & wonderful.

Books with pages are modern day rock stars. Truly.
Someone get me to Bali with a suitcase full of books & nowhere to be.

HACKING HUMANITY

Hands up if you've been to a conference recently & attended a workshop entitled something like Hacking The YouTube Algorithm for Dummies, or Optimising Thumbnails To Drive Views, or Wank Wank Wank... you get my drift.

In our new marketing modernity, we're inundated with magical new platforms & channels. Worlds that exist in the literal ether. It's like we're torn between a hundred different realities that all equal one fallible, imperfect whole in which we all desperately need to look polished & perfect. As humans living with technology 24/7/365, it's as if we're all running to catch up with a bus that left the station before we could hop on board. That damn bus taunts us—going just fast enough that we can't catch it, just slow enough that we're constantly breathing in its dirty fumes.

Yet we keep sprinting. Instead of looking for alternate forms of proverbial transport to catch up, we either throw in the towel or attempt to retrofit our own insufficient engines. I, for one, believe that it's time to find another way forward. Attempting to retrofit traditional ways of life, of communication, & of media into new platforms serves nothing save for memories. We cannot subsist on nostalgia: we must look at where we are now & ensure our gaze is ahead & high.

No one has ever made sense of the future by looking back. No one. Yet when it comes to understanding how technology can enable humanity to be better connected & to do better by the planet & each other, we're breaking our necks in looking behind us. The best thing any of us can do as professionals in any game is to stop, take stock, & move forward, knowing how to harness technology & language to bring about a better tomorrow for us all.

We must know the purpose of our work. And if that work isn't built for driving the betterment of all, then we need to pivot. Hard. Looking through any comment section online, we're all ready & willing to be armchair opinion writers, but we often don't look past a salacious headline. *Purpose* is what we should all be hot & heavy on right now. *Purpose* is the key to hacking all algorithms.

Yep, all of them.

So, as we look ahead & start gathering the bricks & mortar necessary to build a new, strong foundation of communication across borders, cultures, & belief systems, where do we even begin? For me, a line in the sand was drawn on March 15th, 2019.

After the horrific & previously unimaginable terror attack unfolded in Christchurch, New Zealand, the annoyance built around fake news, propagated lies, & algorithms rewarding negative emotive content grew beyond simply annoying. My eyes didn't roll at the click-bait content being served to me in my newsfeed; they wept. A live video feed of the attack, hosted on Facebook, became my end point for all trust in any social media platform or algorithm. Even now, when I talk to others in the social media & digital realms, there's no promise that trust can ever be rebuilt. Surely not in the short term.

From this point on, the way we communicated as people—not simply as professionals who could have predicted something like this—was more around the tech. How in the world can Facebook trawl our newsfeeds for brands & products to give over our content to those with the deepest pockets in the ad-spending world, but can't shut down & get rid of a film of mass murder? Not good enough. Not good enough at all.

What happened after March 15th in New Zealand was strong. Not only did the people of New Zealand band together to help our Muslim whanau, but the government took action. There was no pussyfooting around, no playing hanky-panky-handsy-pansy with pro-gun lobbyists. We didn't molly coddle alt-right-wing idiots. Nope, the government came together to change laws about gun ownership & held Facebook, Google, & other large social media platforms accountable for putting profit & the stirring of white supremacy above safety & betterment.

After March 15th, I took Facebook & YouTube off my phone. From the numbers, it looks like a whole lot of other people did, too. But not nearly enough. We have very short memories & our brains are wired for the next dopamine hit. How do we protect ourselves & generations to come from the harm that's come of opening the world up to digital platforms & AI that are inherently human; & by rights, inherently flawed? How do we tame the Wild West of algorithmic inflammatory content being the best kind of content & protect free speech whilst outlawing hate speech?

Big questions, I know. If I sit and think through potential answers or throw around ideas with colleagues & friends, it's very easy to get lost for hours on the subject & to come out the other side of those lost hours without firm answers. I think that's the most frustrating part of it all, too.

That the people who built these algorithms & these content beasty machines knew from the get-go what they were doing to the wiring of our minds. They knew the implications for good —and ignored the implications for bad as long as they could. All for what? Money? Fame? Who knows; all I know is that we've got some jobs ahead of us to do as a group of professionals with healthy budgets.

When I think about *hacking humanity*, I think about different buckets in which artificial intelligence (AI) is already seeping into our days. From our social media newsfeeds to our Spotify music playlists to our health tracking & fitness modules, we're almost blindly handing over personal choice & data in exchange for ease of navigation when it comes to the absolute glut of content we're faced with daily on our phones, our tablets, our computers, & our TV screens.

We're told that machines are faster, smarter, better than us. But to what extent? Who is defining "better," anyhow? In a time when we're deleting social media apps from our phones in droves, it's apparent that we're all crying out for the bliss of boredom & the creativity found in connection. We're also lacking diversity. The sameness inherent in algorithms that feed us the same stuff time & time again is predisposing us to look only left when we used to take in the world above, below, & to the right of us as well.

The biggest missing link for every social platform that I can see right now is diversity. I'm not talking about the end users, here; most of the time, consumers are last to be asked about what they desire from a platform & are utilised more as test-cases to see how a platform or channel will best deliver stickability (engagement) while maximising potential ad revenue. When I talk about diversity, I mean it's necessary from the conceptualisation of a channel from day dot.

Diversity must be seen as more than simply demographics, too. True diversity spans experience, cognitive nuances, religion, race, socio-economic status, disability, age, gender, sexuality, & personal interests. Promoting inclusivity means building inclusively. To date, the digital profession has been pretty shit at being anything other than male.

To move forward & bridge algorithmic gaps, we must consistently ask questions. We need to be intentional in our curiosity & in how we spend our ad dollars. If we call for change but do not change the way we spend, then the primacy of profit in driving everything we do online in the future will continue. I don't know about you, but as a sappy parent who still watches her child sleeping, I am hell-bent on leaving my daughter a better world.

We must do & be better by & for our young people. We must lead by example. Sometimes, leadership looks large & looming; other times, it says, "Today I will not put all of my money into a giant corporation that sells safety online in return for a higher number on the open market." We as marketers are potent. We as human beings owe it to future generations to ask, & start solving, some of the main problems we wrought & brought upon ourselves by allowing big tech organisations to go unchecked for so long.

I'm keen to understand more about ethics online & in how we build AI moving forward. If I'm honest, as of right now, I definitely don't have all of the answers—in fact, I don't even know how to start asking the right questions in ways that can make lasting & positive change. But I'm learning. I'm fumbling through the process of unknowing & getting comfortable with discomfort in the online arena.

We can afford to be many things in this life, but apathetic is not one of them. We cannot be afraid to have real, deep discourse on the effects of algorithms & social media on our societies. We throw around $10 words willy nilly when we know a few $2 words will suffice in getting the job done. To what end? To dance around subjects that we know won't be easy to solve. But easy isn't how I've ever wanted my life to be—how about you?

Together, if we ask enough of the right questions, we might just start coming up with great ways to move forward collectively. I've started a list; if you've got other questions, please add them below—I've left some blank space for you here:

- Who decides what *ethical* is when it comes to algorithms?
- Where is the line when talking about hate speech & free speech in the same, shallow breath?
- Who decides what *diversity* is when it comes to building platforms?
- What can be defined as good/bad/indifferent when thinking through UX & design for social media channels?
- Do we build for addiction because it's good for the bottom line?
- How do we build for curiosity, creativity, & personal expression?
- Where do we teach our young people about the necessity of deep thought & boredom?

FUCKING UP &
DOING BETTER

B uckle up, this chapter (like 2020 itself!) is going to be a
bumpy ride.

To set the scene a bit: as I write this chapter it's early Sep-
tember of 2020. I wrote most this book (95% of it, to be more
exact) in late 2019, long before a tiny wee virus was on any of
our proverbial radars.

Oh what a time 2019 was. Hindsight is 20/20, for reeeeeeeeealz.
Am I right?

I digress.

Let's talk about unprecedented times for a moment.
2020 is & has been the longest & the fastest & the most up-ended
year of my entire life.
Wait, no let me get this right.
2020 is & has been the longest & the fastest & the most up-ended
year of *all of our lives*.

Now is a time that's got every single human on Earth shook.
Shook to our cores.

And because we're all shook & all of our social media channels are bursting at the seams with mediocre & unchallenged reckons (ahem, opinions are like a**holes, am I right?), we're all looking to connect with each other – but connection seems to be a bit hit & miss as of late when it comes to content, branding, & community engagement.

As individuals, we're searching for folks who can help lead us into a promised-land of 'new normal' that includes things like hugging friends, sitting in the same room with colleagues, & travelling beyond our safe little bubbles. I haven't been home for 16 months now. The borders here in New Zealand aren't looking like they'll be open to my homeland of the USA for a long, long time yet. So, I sit & stare into the wild wonder that is time yet ahead of us & wonder WTAF is going to happen in the days, weeks, months, & years ahead.

As brands, it's almost as if we're adrift.
Should we cut marketing spend?
Should we ramp up marketing activity?
Should we just sit back & listen for a while… or shall we shout into the vacuum & hope to make a ripple of engagement become tantamount to a wave?

All of these questions are valid, important, & individual to each busines, brand, product, & media planner on the planet. Pre-Covid we thought we were really onto something. We had a little recipe for growing the bottom line & it was (ahem, seemingly) fool-proof.

Take one part insight, add in a heaping spoonful of clever content, mix with two parts media spend, & then sprinkle with sassy community management for a ready-made brand strategy.
2020 has taken than strategy, chewed it up.
Spat it out.

And, whilst we are still all trying to figure out a new recipe for success during a time of upheaval at a basic human needs level, some of us have forgotten the basics of connection & interaction that will always be a part of successful marketing & brand building.

I'd like to take this moment, since we all know I've got the time (working from home + pandemic slowdown + all the reckons in my head = plenty of time & inspo to write) to talk about the fine art of fucking up & apologising.

First & foremost it is important to state from the get-go that I am a queen of f*cking up & asking for forgiveness. In fact, if I am working on a project or with a client & I am not making mistakes & asking for forgiveness at some point, then I'm not growing, evolving, or learning. FAIL = First Attempt At Learning in my world, so if I'm grooving, or flying through life & work without any bumps or turbulence – then I know it's time to pack my proverbial bags & start charting a new course.

My most current new course is one in which content becomes less a calorie source for hungry algorithms & more a fountain of emotional tugs & the heartstrings of audiences.

In today's content soaked world, consumers are smarter than we marketers give them credit for – but we don't treat them like they are. I mean, we're living in a time of purpose & meaning. We might be living in THE TIME of purpose & meaning to be exact.

The long & the short of our times is that brands cannot be tone deaf in a time of overwhelming access to tools for listening, data, education, insight, as well as the ability to connect with others 24/7. Making mistakes is normal. Failing is necessary. But f*cking up without doing your homework & expecting impunity is a simple abuse of trust.

So what am I getting at here? Well, I've seen a lot of brands jumping onto cultural memes & moments without having earned the right to. When you get things super-duper-silly wrong as a brand this tells me that there's been a breakdown in understanding how to build & create resonance with your brand whilst connecting this resonance to a higher, organizational purpose.

It is our job as the folks who hold large budgets & thus have overbalanced access to human attention at scale, to put communications into the world that betters humanity. It is not our job to "sell at any cost" & to widen destructive cultural chasms by throwing gasoline on already out of control wildfires.

So, now that we've got that out of the way, let's shift well into gear now & talk about the ethical side of businesses benefitting from cultural memes. To be clear, by *benefit* I loosely mean monetary or positive brand traction & momentum thanks to the usage of the cultural meme or mention of such cultural trend.

So, my main question here is: Is it ever ethical for a business to benefit from a cultural moment in time that was created by & for a community that did not willingly include said brand, product, or offering in it at the time of inception?

My take is that, if a brand has been invited in to the cultural meme & contextual party by the community behind the movement, then that brand can start doing the due diligence necessary to wading into the waters where culture meets capitalism. This is the part where I state clearly that brands must do their homework. Jumping into the aforementioned waters without checking them for depth, sharks, mermaids, or anything else is not cool. If you're going to benefit off of a cultural moment monetarily, then it is imperative that you understand the moment so inherently that there's no question that your brand purpose aligns with the deeper context with the moment being leveraged.

We all know what a rollicking ride of a last 8 months we've all lived through. From a global pandemic to civil tensions to wider discussions on race, gender, privilege & diversity – there should literally not be a single person at the helm of any business (large or small) or decision-making process who can say that they're not "aware" of cultural tensions as they pertain to the moment in time we're all living in right now.

So how can we all do better & what lessons can we learn from this oopsie moment?

I reckon the first thing we can do is not cancel anyone. Cancel culture is rife & means the human aspect of making mistakes cannot be tolerated in a world where mistakes make us who we are. All of the cliches about becoming stronger & doing better by the world through failure & learning happen when we fuck up.

When we see the word FAIL as First Attempt In Learning, then we see the world as a place where we can be novices. We can try new things. Mess up. Apologise heartfully, then move on as better & more compassionate people or businesses. As a movement, cancel culture at it's most shallow is plain & simple yuckiness. I personally will never stand behind a movement by which mistakes spell an end to a person or a brand – especially when the mistakes were made without malice, malintent, or were just plain accidental.

I will state for the record that any person, brand, or product that intentionally aims to hurt, mislead, or pull a quick one over others should be held to account for their actions (or, by rights, inactions). I am a forgiving soul, but let me tell you, this Momma can also hold a grudge better than Elmer's Glue can hold pieces of a broken vase together.

So, in following the whole "not cancelling brands/people/products at the drop of a hat" here are five quick checks all of us can & should do before posting or going live with any culturally explicit campaigns:

Do Your Cultural Homework.

Cultural relevance is of the utmost importance when stepping into the realm of social media & community engagement campaigns. A simple online search will usually leave shit ideas on the shop floor instead of allowing them to be set free to see the light of day online or in other iteration.

If you're super attentive & want to truly understand a cultural moment that we're all living through & that your brand is wanting to leverage off of – treat the moment like a homework assignment that you're super passionate about. Dig deep, get curious, cross-reference a lot of sources.

The lesson for all of us to learn? It's much easier to decide whether or not we should enter a conversation as a brand when we're armed with knowledge. So, dive deeper. Do your cultural homework.

Ask Others.
This one is simple. I know from working in big brands & agencies for a couple decades now that sometimes we get so excited about an idea that our vision about it becomes myopic. When we ask people who aren't in marketing, advertising, or who might think differently to us about an idea (& when we are truly open to constructive feedback), then we grow. Mistakes happen.

They happen more often when we work in vacuums of our own making. So ask others, look beyond arm's length, & be prepared to can an idea if it's not right.

Stick to your purpose.
Every piece of content, every campaign, every official communication that goes out on behalf of a brand not only reflects on the brand itself, but sets up a framework of interpretation for consumers who are on the receiving end of said business communication.

When your campaigns or your content are at odds with your purpose, it's not only off-putting – it breaks down brand trust. We're all guilty of putting out ads simply to fill a media placement or creating "engagement campaigns" to make a spreadsheet look better at the end of the month. The lesson here is that, if we're living our purpose as a business, we'll only ever build trust instead of breaking it through dissonance. Show up as you, always. And, if you haven't been invited into a cultural conversation, it's always a good idea not to jump right on in shouting.

Be Kind.
This article is about kindness. What it's not about is wokeness. Kindness is awareness. And awareness means thinking beyond a singular brand as you hope it might be interpreted in a vacuum. Awareness of the world, humanity, & the community in which you work is of the utmost importance. Now, more than ever. So before signing anything off, all of us should be asking: is this kind to everyone? If the answer is "No," go back to the drawing board.

Apologise Meaningfully When You F*CK UP.
This step in the "fucking up process" is the part where doing better begins. If I was the boss of all the world I would make it a law that PR professionals who work & live to defend brands would never, EVER write apologies on behalf of brands ever again.

There's something about stripping out any kind of true remorse, emotion, or empathy when it comes to the norm of corporate non-apologies that leaves a bad taste in my mouth. I have only ever seen a handful of truly meaningful apologies made by businesses or business people in my lifetime. When the time comes that brands realise the power of owning their fuck ups completely & apologising to the people they've hurt with true care & compassion, we will all truly see a monumental shift in the consumerist paradigm in which we're all living towards community, & optimism.

At this moment in time though, I hope we all take a step back & think longer & more heartfully about what we're suggesting to put into the world. Mistakes, at the worst of times are hard lessons to swallow, but at the best of times they are gifts. Deep reflection often leads to great changes for the better. As we build together & do business together, we must also pay tribute to the moment that we're in.

We've had a bit of a view into a world with less consumerism as we come out of 2020 & a pandemic year that has shifted our global outlooks greatly. Moving back to a buy-buy-buy-buy way of selling & doing business feels dirty & uncaring.

From this moment on we get to see who leads with heart as we forge a new collective "normal." By rights, we'll also clearly see who desperately clings to the idea of "more is better" when more people than ever before have less at the expense of it.

Here's to all of us doing better for each other.
Here's to our new world, re-imagined as one that doesn't need attacking with gusto, but rather that deserves being tended to gently. Like a garden that needs ploughing, watering, preening, & sunlight to grow.

A mantra for us all:
Listen, learn, evolve, grow, repeat.
Listen, learn, evolve, grow, repeat.
Listen, learn, evolve, grow, repeat

Consumers are us.
We are them.
We are all in this together.

#KindnessWarriors, let's do this.

MILLENNIAL
MUFFIN-TOPS

Oh, muffin.

What would any good marketing book in modern times be like without mentioning the most beautifully misunderstood generation of all times (bleurgh, not!): millennials.

What a year it's been for us, too. We've waded knee-deep into the murky waters of professional self-identification—labelled unwittingly as leaders of a wild, unruly younger generation who are currently (or soon to be) taking the workforce by storm. We're all namaste & rose-coloured-glasses. And we're tarred with a brush of brand bed-hopping instead of knuckling down & owning a languishing, lackadaisical loyalty to big business the way our parents did.

This is the point where I need to be completely open & honest with you before we go any further together on this topic: I just squeak in to the millennials category. Just.

And like many folks my age, I've at times felt shame in admitting my true self as part of this new, heathen generation of professionals who are coming into the workforce not only with a bloody good education, but with strong a sense of self-worth.

I often hide my millennial status. Of all the labels I give myself & allow others to stick to me like Post-Its that'll eventually run out of stick, millennial has not been one of them. Especially on LinkedIn or in any professional forum online or offline, where even the mention of being a millennial is met with a hiss & a dismissive gesture*.
*by dismissive gesture, I mean middle finger of death.

I've often avoided millennial conversations at work in the past. Gawd, this sounds tedious & banal even in my own mind whilst I type the words out here on this page, but it's true. I've called myself a Xennial. More times than I'm proud of, too. Why? Well, simply to try to somehow be less millennial than I am. To wash away some of the dust from the bumpy road we've travelled as part of the beta-test generation of Internet users & social media maestros.

I'm tired of hiding who I am.
Screw that.

Here I stand (yes, I am standing—what a weirdo), & proudly admit: Ich bin ein millennial!

As Bob Dylan once crooned (yes, I'm damn well quoting a 1964 Dylan masterpiece here):
Come mothers and fathers
Throughout the land
And don't criticize
What you can't understand
Your sons and your daughters
Are beyond your command
Your old road is rapidly aging
Please get outta' the new one if you can't lend your hand
For the times they are a-changin'…

Right here, right now, and henceforth I shall see myself as an out- &-proud member of the millennial generation. Not as young as

I once was (or hopefully as young as I'll ever be), I am currently servicing a mortgage, working full-time, raising a child, & beautifully embarking on my second marriage. By all accounts, you'd think I was (GASP! HORROR!) old. I kinda am, though. SPOILER ALERT: some millennials are old.

They've been around the traps, lived a few lives, & are now comfortable in their own skin. By rights, there are some beautifully fresh youngins as part of the lumped-together generation I am a part of, too.

But that's neither here nor there... because a millennial I am.

Recently, millennials have come under attack. It appears to be that we're seen as generally lazy. We're believed to be disloyal to corporations (funny that, when they're not loyal to us). And mostly, we're pegged as dreamers. A generation of worker-bees who long to do purposeful work. And by "purposeful," we often mean throwing out the primacy of profit as the shining light of professional success with the corporate bathwater.

Inter-generational bashing by older humans has always been a *thing*. I mean, if older generations didn't drive themselves crazy with narratives around "back in my day those whippersnappers never would've survived!", then what would older generations drive themselves crazy with at all?

In fact, if all of the hard-nosed-corporate die-hards & TV armchair warriors who fear the Internet & social media weren't kicking up a stink about our newly connected & mostly digital age group, I'd be pretty surprised.

Not surprising was a recent case of millennial bashing by someone high in an Australasian muffin management position. Yes, *muffin management*. In short, the General Manager of Muffin Break in Australia had a right good public boo-hoo about millennials.

If my eyes could've rolled out of my head, they might have. In one foul media-heavy swoop, Miss Muffin decided to tar all humans of a certain age range with a brush of selfishness, entitlement, & unworthiness… all because no one was beating down her door anymore, asking for free internships or unpaid work experience.

Let me cut to the chase: the Internet & many fellow millennials went a bit ballistic with this story for a multitude of reasons. First, finger-pointing at millennials is equal parts cringeworthy & foolhardy. It also makes me anxious & giddy. Through foot-stomping attempts by elders to intellectualise an inherent disdain for us new-aged generation of rabble-rousers, I've come to see as clearly as day that strong-arming youth is the last way to entice us to bake muffins for free. We were raised better than that.

The irony of *where* conversations against this way of thinking have been undertaken wasn't lost on me, either. That someone can badmouth an entire generation of people & is now facing backlash on social media just makes me giggle. Oh, the hellish world that we now occupy.

A world in which your job title doesn't make you correct or better than anyone else. A world in which the democratisation of information has helped us all pull together to do better & be better by each other.

Oh my soul, this lady was so lost in how she went about bemoaning the loss of free labour. The sad part is that she's not alone in her thoughts. All you need to do is hop online & search "Millennials" & you'll be served up millions of mentions that brand us as kids who grew up on participation medals—afraid to win, though not willing to lose. Older generations have always feared/questioned/looked on in disbelief at the changing tides of younger generations; this isn't new. This is inherently human.

What is new, though, is that we younger folks (ahem, millennials & beyond) are armed with a whole lot of information that previous generations weren't armed with. We've watched our grandparents & our parents. We've learned from them. We know what we want to be. And what we're willing to put up with to get there.

We know our rights.
We know what we think is right. We have the right to choose.

Who we are is not denoted by our position descriptions. We are not words written on paper by someone else. We're not cogs in wheels that lead to nowhere. Nope. Not us.

We're a generation built on expectations of creating a better world. We're dreamers, hard workers, & open-hearted labourers. But we ARE NOT a free-for-all.

I know a lot about millennials, and here are a few things I know for certain:

We know better.
In her rant to the media, Muffin Break's GM reckoned that entitled millennials have been given an "inflated" sense of self-importance due to all of these newfangled apps that connect them to the interwebs. Apparently, young people who talk to other young people get ideas. Unfiltered ideas. Powerful ideas. Geeky ideas. All of these ideas aren't eventuating into work ethic, though, are they?

These young whippersnappers with all their newfangled ideas are no longer beating down her door or forging a path to Muffin Break's counter begging for unpaid work experience to advance their careers. "There's just nobody walking in my door asking for an internship, work experience or unpaid work, nobody," she lamented. Publicly. Team, she said this to the media.

My first response? Well, after picking my jaw up off the floor, I laughed. Surely she's somehow, accidentally been eating one of those *funny muffins* & she's not thinking clearly. My second thought, after realising that marijuana doesn't cause the kind of daftness she's spouting, was, "Good golly y'all, never in all of my millennial years would I consider working for free at making muffins (or selling cars, or paper pushing, or coffee making, or anything really)."

I've always had to pay the rent, put food on the table, raise my family. Cold hard cash is needed for that. The antiquated idea working your way up a ladder still needs to equate to a living wage. Ladders don't pay the rent if climbing up each rung puts you further down the breadline.

We know better now, too. We also know that underpaying people (which Muffin Break has apparently been known to do in the past) or not paying them at all is illegal. Ahem, illegal. We're not selfish for wanting to be paid for our time & our toil —no matter how important or inane. Our non-millennial parents taught us better. Society taught us better & wrote policies to protect us from this kind of thinking. We want to work hard. We're crazy about the mahi. And for it, we ask to be paid appropriately. That's the exchange: not all for nothing. Thanks to those who came before us, we know this for certain.

Exploitation is on display.
Exploitation & exasperation; this is exactly what this GM & her cohorts who shake their fists at the *youth of today* are advocating. Folks who used to intern for free were usually either able to be supported by their parents (the lucky ones) or were so desperate that they saw no other way than exploitation to get a foot in the door. We know that a lot of people are willing to put up with exploitation because they're desperate and fearful and really need a job.

Data also tells us that, on average, unpaid internships leave most young people $6,000 out of pocket. Let me just remind us all, too, that most internships aren't for the big time. We're not talking internships that lead to high-stakes here; those are usually reserved for a very upper-class & very privileged few. We're talking about muffins here, folks. Baked goods & tasty treats en masse.

The mindsets of leaders who promote old-school views of just-feel-lucky-to-be-chosen-and-do-what-you're-told-kid are exasperating, at best, for an older millennial like myself. I've never, not once, considered working for a business or corporation for free. Why? It's take/take on behalf of said corporate without any give. Value needs to be exchanged in one way or another. Believe me, I worked for almost nothing when I was of intern age. Let me be clearer: I worked my ass off for a tiny pay packet that I collected monthly. My pay barely covered gas in my car & rent, but gosh, I was proud of the money in the bank. Why? Because I earned that, damnit. I worked long hours. I made friends with colleagues. My job became a source of pride. And the pay, though crazy low (even for the time), sufficed. Could I have done the job without pay? Nope. Never in a hundred years.

If maligning a generational workforce based on apathy around killing off a value exchange between employee & employer is a thing now, then I'm going to wave my millennial flag daily. Not paying people for work is exploitation. Having to continually repeat this is exasperating.

My Snowflake generation.
Older generations seem to hold this weird belief that all millennials believe we'll be CEO in five years.

Really, though, who says all (or any) of us want to be CEO anymore? The climb just doesn't seem worth it if you end up living in fear of the changing whim of stakeholders, shareholders, or anyone holding your mental health hostage. We've seen work burn our parents out. We've seen the climb take over lives. And, we've learned. Kinda. We've also, even in our youth, burned out too. We don't need to define ourselves by our position descriptions anymore.

We are not words on paper devised by imperfect middle managers who, even with the best of intentions, still see us as numbers on an org chart. We're alive in a time when the democratisation of information, news, & creativity is built into the fiber of our beings. We want to work hard. We want to make the world a better place. And we want to be able to live on a decent wage.

The benefit of youth is the ability to dream without bounds. We are the people who lap up content from people like Brené Brown, Simon Sinek, Hannah Hart, & Glennon Doyle. We look up to people who believe in the future & in the good we can do to heal a planet that a more corporate world misused prior to us. We are self-starters & we dive deep into learning through novels, podcasts, deep reports, popular culture, community projects, & documentaries that we're planning on writing. We know better than to chase dollars over experiences.

All in all, we know better than to hurt others for the sake of the bottom line. We know we get ONE GODDAMN LIFE, & to live it fully, we need to work for the greater good. Are we selfish? Ahem, we're human. So sometimes, yeah. But we're also not going to be duped into scrubbing muffin tins for anyone for less than what our time is worth. Unlike the icing on a lemon-glazed treat, our generation of snowflakes isn't melting anytime soon.

My take on millennials is simple. We're just like all the other generations that came before us—but we're connected to more. Tethered to it, seemingly. The pressures generations before us faced, we face now. But differently. We're still trying to find relevance in the world. We're rushing headlong into a world in which we now need to reverse the effects of global warming. We know we need to do more, better.

We also know what our hearts desire. Doing business with millennials (ahem, with any woke or waking humans) isn't hard.

All you need to do is:
Put people before percentages & profit.
Put heart-counts before headcounts.

When this happens, most people (not just millennials, Gen Z, etc.) will show you loyalty like you've never seen before. When we believe in a mission, in an action, in something better— you'll see the hard yards we're willing, able, & capable of shining through. Inked in positive outcomes for your bottom line.

Actions speak louder than words (remember that one?): we believe in this to our goddamn core.

Care about us, care about our dreams & aspirations, too.
When we care, we'll ride to the end of the universe in a broken-down starship to grow a business.
When we don't? We move on.
Fair enough, too, right?

Snowflakes? Yeah, nah.
More like caring humans who want to do well by family, friends, society, business, nation, & planet.

Millennials, you're okay with me.
And wow, with all of this muffin talk, I'm hungry now.
Anyone know where I can get a snack...?

LINKEDOUT: QUITTING SOCIAL MEDIA FOR GOOD

E
arlier this year, UK company LUSH (yes, the bath bomb brand that I cannot walk past without having either my daughter or my wife—or both—beg to go in) told the world that they would soon be "switching up social." And by switching things up, they meant getting the hell outta Dodge.

In a statement across channels—LOL, yes, ironically social media channels—LUSH took a bold first step, bidding adieu to big social media platforms that were no longer performing on the *social* premise of social media. Social media has increasingly become a fire-hydrant delivery mechanism for a torrent of shoddy, at best, ads.

Brands are paying bajillions of dollars for flashes of reach & very little true engagement while believing sweet-fix metrics are the answer to shouting louder than the next competitor. As of this moment in time, social media big-boys are offering very little when it comes to true community building or brand return. LUSH's move is one that other brands are bound to follow. Increasingly, businesses are paying to fight algorithms

197

for space & attention. Cut-through? Yeah, nah. Consumers have cottoned on to shouty digital tactics. They're blind to anything that isn't inherently valuable, personalised, & contextual.

By saying what many of us are already thinking (that social media is actually making it harder for all of us to connect to each other directly), LUSH peeled back a layer of the banality that social media marketing has become. Increasingly, the lazier marketers amongst us have stopped asking questions & simply opened their wallets & budget lines to the main platforms. Why? Well, mostly because it's easy. Also, because we've put ethical marketing & the cult of curiosity behind us in favour of what's simpler to understand on the surface.

We're spoon-fed dreams of amazing business results & golden eggs, sunny side up. But I can tell you one thing for certain: the time to dig deeper & turn towards our own platforms, ideas, & data management is now. Believing in "success metrics" that have been proven to be fudged time & time again, we blindly trust in platforms that commoditise human attention, but that

pay no attention to humanity itself. My heart breaks for it!

When did a thoughtless like, comment, love-heart, or share come to be a measure of success? When did we stop investing in humanity & storytelling over dull clicks that lead to nowhere? Strategy is not found in spots & dots on a media recommendation; it is carefully crafted around human insight & strong stories that matter. We seem to have been blinded (blindsided, perhaps?) by the shiny metrics of reach & engagement. The good news is that we're becoming more & more woke as a professional cohort. We're finding our cores, looking for purpose, & pushing the brands we work with to do the same.

Across the interwebs, LUSH has riled up a lot of anger &

angst amongst so-called social media gurus. They're seeing red, Team. My recommendation to the soothsayers on shaky ground is this: Namaste, my friends. Namaste. Let's all take a deep breath, reassess, & then rock into how we move forward in ways that better society & drive the purpose of our organisations. In the wake of the disgusting, cowardly attack on Christchurch where the murders of 50 people were live-streamed on Facebook, brands need to do better for & by their customers. And sometimes, *doing better* means taking a good, hard look at the communications we're putting into the world & questioning the places in which we're distributing them.

Those amongst us who have taken to being 100% okay with wading knee-deep into paid advertising that is foundationally cemented in sponsored posts, collection ads, mid-roll interruptions, & interactive whatsamathingies must now start rethinking why, how, where, & on what customers will spend their money. We must think harder about serving our customers—not patting ourselves on the back for paying for reach.

Yet people shake their fists at me when I talk like this. Change is fucking scary. Standing up for something that might be better for our customers but forces us to take a hit in the profit department is even fucking scarier. Does that mean status quo is the only way forward? That's not up to me to decide

—but I bet you can guess how I'd answer that question.

I'm not saying stop the train at the station & put it out with the other rusty has-beens. Should we still invest in social media marketing? Yeah, I think we should. To an extent.

As someone who's worked in social media since working in

social media was a thing, I get it. I see, feel, & have experienced the beauty of social in changing the lives of customers for the better & in opening conversations where before there was only one point of view being shared.

However, I see LUSH's side of things, because I remember those good 'ol days of social media where the SOCIAL aspect was what made all of the connectedness between consumers & brands beautiful.
Now, though, it is time for all of us to start critiquing the nature & the quality of what we're served (& what we're serving) on social.

From the moment brands started trying to outbid each other for a share of our wallets & attention spans, we've become data points, our humanity seemingly forgotten. Digital pollution is real. We've a glut of soulless content being thrown into our lives, & trends seem to be that we're disconnecting more while opting for online experiences that are individually tailored to our own needs & wants.

We're also facing bigger issues than a company that sells yummy-smell-good-products going off of Instagram & Facebook. We've yet to tackle ethical marketing on these platforms. We've yet to consider how much data & information we're giving up as businesses to platforms that aren't truly concerned with our purposes. We've yet to flex our collective muscles in demanding the major social media players put money into protecting the humans they so desperately need to keep on their sites. The good news is that governments are getting involved now.

Rules will be put in place, mandating safety & the

distribution of factual information over the misleading.

Don't get me wrong, here: I always have been quite the fangirl for social media. I love the democratisation of connectedness & of creating content that can be shared far & wide (or not at all). Social is a great tool for driving business & conversations, when used with good intentions. But we're living in a time where bad actors & brands with budgets begging to be spent in our timelines need to be reined in. LUSH's move to lessen time & resource on social media is only the beginning.

As I see it, until the main channels put money & effort into creating truly safe spaces & until we as global citizens can value metrics beyond a shallow like or share as measures of success, then we can change the game by not playing it.

If everyone is just going to accept the status quo, then nothing will change. And change is what is needed. From a brand perspective, LUSH still has people ready to talk & interact—just in a one-to-one way that doesn't originate from a social media channel. Email, DM, live chat, & (shock/horror) phone calls still remain.

Businesses spend the dollars that the social platforms are after. By rights, it is brands that stand in a prized position: businesses can change the world for the better. First, though, we need to start looking beyond ROI & bottom line as measures of success. As we move forward into a time when generations growing up will never know a world without connected technology, it is on us right here & right now to look beyond the sweet fix of shiny reach numbers & dive deeper. It is on us to do better.

While it might not make sense for all brands to quit social

media, LUSH as a brand seem to be putting their money where their heart is. And if that's the case, I'm all for it.

LEAN OUT

The 2013 release of Sheryl Sandberg's novel Lean In was a coup for professional women. It also started a slang revolution that has taken the marketing world by storm: we lean into every goddamn thing these days. But when she wrote her book, Sandberg's intention wasn't to have me rolling my eyes 6 years later every time some hyped-up agency suit said 80 words when they could've made the same point in 5.

Nope, she wasn't intending for us to lean in to target audiences, or to lean into custom audience segmentation. While she did (& still does) have most of us leaning in to colloquialisms at scale, what her book really did at the time was light a fire for a lot of women in business who were bloody tired of manspreading, mansplaining, & man-anything that didn't lift the voices & confidence of female professionals.

Chapters focused on societal norms that doubled (& sometimes tripled, quadrupled...) as confidence breakers. In her chapter 'Sit at The Table,' I found myself nodding along to the book while I read it. In it, I saw myself: I saw just how often I declined compliments around brilliant work I'd delivered because *that's just not what is expected of a professional woman.* The same chapter stung when I saw myself again in the stories of other women who waited for years upon years to try their hands at new roles —women who believed they needed to be 100% qualified to try anything new. Only to be overshadowed by men who some-times had only a hope in hell & maybe 40% of the key skills needed to take a leap up the ladder. Holy sheep-shit, Batman. I leaned waaaaaaaaaaay into the stories Sheryl told.

While I was reading *Lean In*, I remember feeling less empowered than I thought I should. I also remember feeling a mixture of shame & guilt for not standing up for myself more. For not being more steadfast in my decisions to try new things without hav-ing to have huge safety nets below me. In 'The Myth of Doing it All,' I had to put the book down. I knew in my heart of hearts that the last thing I ever wanted to do in life was IT ALL. In fact, from the time I was a little girl, I've had some pretty focused—yet super broad—goals that I let slip aside for fear of not doing it all.

The things I was focused on as a kid? Being happy, being curious, being adventurous, & most importantly being loved & loving. When I started to climb proverbial invisible corporate ladders, I lost my confidence with each rung I climbed. I even met other women who tried their damndest to knock me down or off the ladder completely. Sometimes we women are the worst people when it comes to lifting other women, aye? I've seen horrible bullying by women towards women. In fact, this kind of bully-ing is the absolute worst because we all know what we're up against.

There's no pretending we're unaware of the shame, guilt, & powerlessness that women are born into daily, thanks to our societal structures. I've seen jealousy, pride & almost all of the 7 Deadly Sins be thrown at an already laden-down human being for sport. Shame being shot out of a t-shirt cannon into crowds willy nilly—but this isn't rock 'n roll, my friends. This is taking pain & thinking you can share it or divest yourself of it by push-ing it onto others. This is a journey into the dark, cavernous hole of self-righteous assholery in which we attempt to break a per-son simply for the sake of it. Gross. This is simply gross. We need to do better by & for each other.

While it wasn't what she intended, over time, *leaning in* became a washed-out mantra for aggression, while simultaneously being watered down to be a catch-all for any & everything anyone wanted it to mean. One time, in the middle of a big campaign pitch, a male agency suit actually said to a room full of women, "Lean into the idea, ladies, lean into the sales." I died a little in that moment—& mid-death, left the room, shaking my head at the inanity of said suit's comment. What the fuck, dude. WHAT. THE. FUCK.

Thinking about this book & mantras—I really wanted to offer you, dear reader, something that is actually helpful to you in the office & beyond. To do this, I did one helluva deep dive into the writings & beliefs of strong women leaders who I think are badasses. Beyond Sheryl Sandberg, I looked to Arianna Huffington, Oprah Winfrey, Maya Angelou, Joan Withers. And even though there's a whole lot of hustle, confidence, & taking up space with all of these women, one thing that all of them seem to have in common isn't *leaning in*; rather, it's knowing when to *lean out*.

What do I mean by *leaning out?* Well, at the core of this belief is the fact that, as women, we need to hustle twice as hard to be taken seriously in corporate environments. This isn't a complaint: this is a fact. We have to retrain ourselves to speak up, to call out sexist bullshit without being afraid of reprisal, to take up space at tables that are usually surrounded by men. At times, it's exhausting having to manage the egos & feelings of the men around us. It's even more exhausting trying not to offend said fellas. On top of tip-toeing or changing the way we are to look or come across more traditionally male, we have to do our jobs. We also raise families, run households, nurture relationships, & (more often than not) keep the world spinning on its axis.

At some point, we're going to break.

For all the leaning in, we must also know when to lean out.

Sometimes the lean out is simply to right our balance. If we go too far in, we could end up falling right on our faces. No one's going to catch us, either. It's up to all of us as individuals to notice when we're leaning too far in one direction & to right the ship. *Leaning out* is a way for us to take control of our professional conversations.

When we can take the time to survey a room & understand nuanced situations instead of going hell for leather into a confrontation, we're already the person with the upper hand. I should note, upper hand here might mean that we're able to be more present, able to be more empathetic, or simply that we're the more powerful person in an argument—I'm okay with all three of these happening one at a time or all at once.

To me, *leaning out* is about not buying into the bullshit. From the moment that people started to commandeer & re-define leaning in, leaning out is how I've tried to live my life. The step-back. The step-away, the step-out. The taking of time to really look at an issue from all angles & to redefine how I see myself moving through this world. No matter your background, your age, or how you define yourself on a spectrum of otherness or alignment with a crowd, we are all players in an infinite game of connection, growth, & consciousness. If we're consistently spending all of our energy on leaning in one direction, we forget to look the opposite way. We forget that there's value in otherness & we anticipate only what our biases can see in the most myopic of ways.

Case in point: after reading *Lean In*, I started to be much more intentional in the way I took up space & spoke in meetings. I started to use my mind, my voice, & my potency in ways that I was previously fearful to. For people who know me, I can picture you giggling right now. I've never been anyone's doormat, & I've never gone quietly from a fight that was worth fighting. Yet I tempered my ideologies to fit the men around me.

I made my voice quieter & my body smaller. Once I felt a certain kind of permission at scale, I started to undo all of my self-policing. Let me tell you, it's taken years to even become aware of moments that still exist, when I give my power over to others simply for fear of being seen as bolshy, bossy, or bitchy. These moments happen less & less frequently now because the permission I give myself doesn't come from the words of other people anymore—it comes from within.

Whether I *lean in* or *lean back*, I make the call now. As professionals in an industry that's fast moving & still very set in its ways, it's imperative that we all allow others to own their potent power. It's crucial that we rise by lifting others through our work & the stories we help others to put into the world. You wouldn't think so, but as marketers, it is up to us to do better by everyone: the oppressed, the powerful, those on the edge. We can make change happen daily in small ways, or in big bangs thanks to even bigger budgets looked over by brave changemakers.

What are some secrets to *leaning out* that I've learned as a slightly cynical—yet always optimistic—older millennial marketer?

First & foremost, no matter how busy you are, how many projects you've got on, how many awards adorn your mantelpiece (reminding you, constantly of your brilliance), you must know yourself. You must know yourself well enough to set boundaries & stick to them fastidiously. Be a bulldog or a butterfly; however you protect your own wellbeing, do that. You must also know that your passions, your gut feelings & the love you put into the world matter more than anything.

Know thyself, & in doing so, trust thyself. You can summit any mountain if you take it one step at a time. The art of *leaning out* is an unending journey towards being your most complete & confident self. To bring your best superpowers to the boardroom or a client lunch, you need only be comfortable in your own skin, & in your own scope of knowing. With all this knowledge combined, you'll be one helluva force to be reckoned with on all levels.

After you find out who you are, or even whilst you're doing this, it is imperative to be open to finding wonder in others. Sure, spending time on numero uno is of the utmost importance, but being able to step outside of your own frame of reference to look someone else in the eye & see the passion they see is akin to magic. Actual, sparkly, pie-in-the-sky, happy magic. I have always been much better at finding wonder in others that I have been in recognizing it in myself—the two are not mutually exclusive. Not at all.

However, knowing that every person has a story that is just as valid, nuanced, & important as your own makes navigating the world much easier. Especially in professional settings. Case in point: I am *that person* in my friendship group who can walk into a room filled with people—strangers & friends alike—& walk out of the same room knowing the deepest secrets of passions of those around me. This happens a lot when I go to parties where I am the sober driver & everyone else is a bit tiddly. There's literally nothing like alcohol for loosening up the story machine.

Sometimes being super approachable is a heavy weight—but for the most part, it is upon the stories of others that the strength in my wings is built. It is because of the trust others have gifted me in being able to listen to them & hear them that I am strong enough to fly on my own. Knowing others is, essentially, the best tool for better knowing yourself. We're all so different, there's no denying that. But when you start to really lean out & lean back around others, it's amazing how quickly they lean in to you. Trust, rapport, connection. This is all built over time. There's no magic algorithm or hack for winning friends & influencing people in the long run. The simplest way to be awed by the world is to allow yourself to be in awe of others.

Lastly, & most importantly, once you know yourself & open your heart to finding wonder in others, you can start to look at your impact in the world. And you can be damn proud of it. All big changes start small. Success in terms of how we impact our communities, our colleagues, our families, & beyond isn't quantifiable in numbers alone. As marketers & as professionals, we honestly have the ability to change the world through the decisions we make every day. While you might not be CMO or CDO in your business or in a position to drastically change the way your business works with big tech companies or governments, you still have a sphere of influence that matters. We all do. This is the lean in. When it comes to how we see our sphere of influence & when it comes to dialing up the optimism in bit-sized portions, this is our *lean out*. We are all valid, potent beings. Unlocking who we are at different stages of our lives is how we unlock our potential as a species. Challenges to our thoughts, our preconceived notions, & our in-built biases are always challenges well undertaken.

Sometimes, sure, we need to take up a lot of space at the table. We need to speak when it feels like we might vomit from nerves, & we need to act when we're scared shitless to do so. But remember the other side of the hustle: the slow down. Without both, we're simply yin without yang. We're Elton without Bernie. If you take anything away from this book at all, may it be to perfect the art of *leaning out*. If enough of us do so, we might just re-balance the scale. We might just see better work, better results, & better looked-after colleagues because of it.

FUCK YOU, MARKETING! (PS I LOVE YOU)

So there you have it: 60,000 words (give or take) that stand not only as a gritty rallying cry & sharp-toothed love letter to marketing as a profession—but a call to action for all of us to take our marketing hats off every once in a while when we're planning advertising with an end goal of cutting through the noise & being memorable (hell, even being likable!) to the people we're keen to do business with.

It's not rocket science, marketing. It's not even data science —though we spend a shit-ton on number crunchers & insight analysts who tell us that marketing is, in fact, all about data. I'd argue that the best marketing is another kind of science all together. Or rather, an alchemy of sorts. Marketing is an ever-evolving landscape of medium & culture. It is a bringing together of medium & culture at a macro level. For any marketing to work, you must aim to drive impact through storytelling, emotion, connection, & purpose. Of course, you can plan, build pillars, create brand books around tone & values all you want —this is definitely great for your internal teams to understand a brand's aura. But there's only so much of defining your own brand that you can actually do. Today, your brand is what your customers tell you it is. If you're not listening to them, you will forever be on the back foot. Forever inches away from truly connecting with the people you long to connect with.

Also, there's data. Big data. Small data. Identity-driven data. Geolocation... ERMERGHERD, we've got data pouring out of our ears! But data is not a magic bullet unless you know how to make it magical. You can cut your data, segment your audiences, & try to out-clever your competitors all you want, but until you have a good story that connects with your audience & products that matter to them, well, you're simply spinning wheels for the sake of motion.

Motion ain't always progress. Success in the marketing game, it seems, is in dire need of a freshening up. The channels we use to connect to people may change, but our basic human need for telling & taking in stories has never changed. It's heightened now. It's imperative.

Marketing has a lot to answer for, too. In a time before social media & before the democratization of content sharing, brands could talk at us instead of to us. I always pictured the ad men of the past as some guy on top of a skyscraper with a megaphone, shouting down at people as they crossed busy streets in metropolitan areas.

We didn't have megaphones then, so all we could do was ignore the din or shout back into the wind, where our voices were carried away before the man in a wool suit atop the building could hear our feedback. It seems to me that this is exactly how the world of modern marketing worked until about two decades ago. We were a bit easier to dupe, pre-internet, weren't we? Actually, "dupe" isn't the right word. We as a mass of consumers lived our lives & believed what we wanted to, disbelieved what we wanted to. It's only more recently that most of humanity now communicates directly with a brand. Or many brands. Or no brands at all.

Marketing, it seems, has become a study in allowing others to define your brand. This is a good thing, I reckon. Those professionals who learn to listen more than they speak (or otherwise still try to reach for a megaphone atop a skyscraper to shout below at random foot traffic) will be those who successfully survive. Entire businesses have been built on listening to consumers. Gone are the days when you needed to own a lot to be a lot as a business. Look at Uber, AirBnB, & all social media platforms. None of these mega-companies started with more than an insight, an idea, & a way to disrupt the world as it has been for decades.

When I think about marketing pulling the proverbial wool whilst also pulling our legs, I think about the fitness tracker on my wrist. Along with eating breakfast (ahem, spoiler alert: it's not actually *the most important meal of the day*—that's a marketing line) & drinking 8 glasses of water, we've been told that we need to take 10,000 steps a day to maintain our health.

I can't tell you how many times I've walked around the house an extra two times to hit my daily 10,000 steps. At one point, I was so obsessed with hitting my 10K a day that I'd get up before dawn & walk like a mad fool to beat the day of sedentary meeting time ahead of me. I should say now: taking 10,000 steps a day is good! Moving your body is inherently better than not.

That said, we're entranced by the number—10,000 steps! Have you gotten your steps in today? Ah, I see you're taking the stairs! Yasssss to getting your steps in. Let me tell you: this is a complete & utter fucking ruse. You see, in 1965, a Japanese pedometer company came out with a product called "The 10,000-Step Meter." The name was chosen for the product because the Japanese character for 10,000 looks kind of (at a freaking stretch) like a man walking. There you go, Team. We've been hoodwinked for over 50 years now into believing something that was based on no more than someone in marketing deciding their product would sell better with a story attached to it.

I should note here: new scientific studies show that most people only need to take 4,400 steps a day for health benefits. But me? I'm brainwashed. It's 10K or nada. There's no in-between when it comes to active me & lazy-ass-on-the-couch-with-Doritos me. But hey, what's life without balance?

As I draw this book to a close, I'd like to simply ask that you, dear reader, do a bit of namaste soul searching & really start asking questions about what you're doing, why you're doing it, & who you're doing it for. Every piece of communication we put out into the world must be purposeful & driven by a singular purpose that rises above & beyond the primacy of profit. We need to all take a step back & ask why we're putting such a glut of content out into the world that has a high probability of never being seen, & an even higher probability of never making the world better for all of us. With great budget lines comes great responsibility. Now is a time to stop filling voids simply because you can buy a cheap reach. We must work harder to do less, better. We must be better.

It is now that the tides are turning; whether or not you're prepared for the ensuing waves is up to you. When looking at your customers, see the best in them. People are more than data points; treat them & their lives accordingly. Now is a time ready-made for hacking. We must hack kindness & empathy for good—not algorithms for gain. I am bored to tears of the people who are hell-bent on telling me I must learn to hack algorithms & how to optimize thumbnails. Nope! That shit is shitty. Plain & simple.

Also, remember to be kind. Kindness is a magical elixir of success that many people forget to mix into their professions when they get caught up in the day-to-day fray of working life. With radical candor at the core of how we comport ourselves, we'll ensure customer experience becomes a relational interaction that drives long-term brand love & affinity.

The most important thing we can do as marketers?
We must remember to tell good stories. Great stories. Stories that matter. Stories that are easy for people to pass on & re-tell themselves. You heard it here, folks: learn to spin one helluva yarn & you'll always, always, always be at the top of any game you choose to make your own.

In summary, I love & lament our current marketing landscape in equal measure.

Fuck you, marketing.
P.S. I love you
Epilogue

Lorem ipsum dolor sit amet, consectetur adipiscing elit, sed do eiusmod tempor incididunt ut labore et dolore magna aliqua. Ut enim ad minim veniam, quis nostrud exercitation ullamco laboris.

AFTER, WORDS

I wrote this 98% book in 2019.
A world that COVID-19 had yet to take over.
A world that was as hope-filled as I was hopeful.
A world in which businesses truly belived in doing better for
the envoronment, for human rights, for indness, & for building
strong communities.

But, then 2020 happened.
The world stopped.
The world changed faster than ever.
The world was thrown off of its axis.

Or, so it seemed.

In relation to the stories I've told in this book, the morals &
ethics remain regardless of COVID-19 or who we are today because of it.

Marketing & advertising can change the world for the better. We
can all change the world for the better.
Are you in?

ACKNOWLEDGEMENTS

Sometimes, in moments of complete silence (or in louder moments while I'm out running & blasting Radiohead), I take stock of my life.

I count my blessings & think deeply about all of the people in my life who have supported me over the years. It's in these moments that I remember my reason.

I remember my purpose. I remember that all of us - even me - are worthy, whole, & able to make dreams & live them.

Writing this book was a salve.
A healing. A coming back to myself.

Therefore, I'd like to thank every person who has played a part in my journey for your contribution. The good, the bad, & the magical all add up to a life fully lived.

It's because of you that I am me.

To my family, friends, & beloveds.
Thank you for being the beat of my heart.

ABOUT THE AUTHOR

Cassie Roma

 Cassie Roma is a Kindness Warrior & one helluva heavy-hitter. Originally from California, she's spent the past 17 years in New Zealand building a formidable career in the media, marketing, & advertising world.

Passionate about creative content, social media strategy, the influencer economy, & storytelling across mediums both emerging and traditional, Cassie has literally lived & breathed the digital revolution.

Whilst she has spent the majority of her career working in & with large corporates, she is now a fully-fledged entrepreneur, working as both Founder & Director of CR&Co, a game-changing consultancy & multi-media business built around the impactful areas of brands where creativity, content, & code collide.

Before the launch of CR&Co, Cassie held high-ranking roles at businesses like Air New Zealand, ANZ Bank, The Warehouse Group, Mighty River Power & New Zealand Media & Entertainment (NZME) where she crafted & drove the content marketing, social media, & storytelling strategies of some of the most innovative & iconic brands globally & across the APAC region.

Cassie has been awarded & recognised globally as a thought leader in the fields of digital marketing, social media marketing, storytelling for brands, & the anthropological power of brand in the lives of consumers.

She's also an author, keynote speaker, TEDx speaker, professional coach, & mentor.

She's also one big bundle of positive energy fuelled by the belief that great corporate culture is built on a foundation of empathy, insight, & kindness!

Beyond the office, Cassie spends her free time working on projects that she's passionate about – most of which aim to lift others through education, diversity, & action. Cassie is a proud member of the LGBTQIA+ community & speaks often on topics that include Pride & empowering women in the workplace.

At home, Cassie is a proud momma to a brilliant teenaged daughter, & wife to her soulmate.

She loves getting outdoors while soaking up some sunshine & revelling in stolen moments with loved ones.

Made in the USA
Monee, IL
12 February 2021

59236886R00128